Praise for *Paid to Piss Peo[ple Off]*
Book 1 PEACE, Book 2 PORN, B[...]

"Barry Lynn does it again! This tale of his life and [...] inspiring and energizing as all the hard work he's [...]. You will be entertained and occasionally horrified by the people and institutions he has taken on. He shows how real activism works and how you can do the work too!"

—Thom Hartmann, progressive national radio and television host and best-selling author

"Barry Lynn brilliantly expresses his ideas which he delivers with wit, humor, and panache. If this book is in your hands, you're lucky. Open it and start reading. You'll be glad you did."

—Lewis Black, comedian

"Barry Lynn has been a tenacious advocate for peace and justice. I am glad that he has gotten around to writing this memoir of his extraordinary life."

—Pat Schroeder, former Congresswoman from Colorado

"Barry Lynn has created an important and beautiful literary treasure. Lynn is brilliant and courageous, a key figure in the amnesty and peace movements who has written an unforgettable portrait of a generation in turmoil. This is a fascinating history lesson told with wit, honesty, and grace."

—Ron Kovic, Vietnam veteran and author of *Born on the Fourth of July*

"Barry Lynn is a national treasure and *Paid to Piss People Off* perfectly captures his trajectory. He built a career out of poking holes in hypocrisy and religious zealotry using an artful blend of substance, humor, and incisive wit. This book captures the unvarnished essence of the Rev. Barry Lynn, one of the most important voices of his generation."

—Wade Henderson, former President of the Leadership Conference on Civil and Human Rights

"Lucky Barry Lynn for leading such a fun life. And lucky for all of us for him to have led such a purposeful life. Decades of work on civil rights, peace, and true religious freedom make me proud to be one of his fellow travelers."

—Bill Press, former co-host of CNN's Crossfire and award-winning author

"Barry Lynn is one of the rare people who recognize the deep connection between social justice, music, comedy, and film. He understands and never waivers in his support of folks on the margins of society. I think he likes us more than the powerful politicians he has worked with all these years. Barry is a gem; his words, truth to power. These three volumes are thrilling."

—Mary Gauthier, Grammy nominated songwriter and author of *Saved by A Song*

"I observed Barry Lynn doing the difficult dance between faith and social policy for three decades, regretfully mainly as his ideological nemesis. Too late in life I concluded that he was mostly right and I was mostly wrong. This memoir helps me make up for lost time and might allow others to do the same."

—The Rev. Rob Schenck, director of the Bonhoeffer Institute and former leader in the anti-abortion movement

"Barry Lynn has always been a powerful speaker and leader of progressive causes, and a strong advocate for women's privacy and bodily integrity. This book is a clarion call to the next generations to never give up on fighting hard for what is right."

—Kim Gandy, Past President of the National Organization for Women and current President of the National Network to End Domestic Violence.

Paid to Piss People Off:
Book 1 PEACE

Barry W. Lynn

BLUE
CEDAR
PRESS

Blue Cedar Press
Wichita, Kansas

Blue Cedar Press
P.O. Box 48715
Wichita, KS 67201

Visit the Blue Cedar Press website: *www.bluecedarpress.com*

10 9 8 7 6 5 4 3 2 1
First edition April 2023
ISBN: 978-1-958728-08-6 (paper)
ISBN: 978-1-958728-09-3 (ebook)

Cover design by Barry W. Lynn, Joanne Lynn, and Gina Laiso.
Cover photo: Christina Lynn at anti-draft rally. Source: Author's collection.
Interior design by Gina Laiso, Integrita Productions.
Editors Laura Tillem and Gretchen Eick.

Library of Congress Control Number (LCCN): 2023931758

Printed in the United States of America

Note: Images are from Author's personal collection unless otherwise identified.

TABLE OF CONTENTS

INTRODUCTION

In Washington, DC hundreds of Davids try to slay Goliaths, Goliaths such as: "the military-industrial complex" President Eisenhower warned the nation about when his terms as president ended. Or Big Pharma and the insurance industry that keep health care costs in the U.S. the highest in the world. Or "Dark Money" that since the 2006 *Citizens United* Supreme Court decision has allowed billionaires to sway our elections. Consider the prison industrial complex that has made the U.S. the biggest jailer in the world. Or the Religious Right and its allies in Congress waging their "culture wars" against public schools and concepts of human rights.

Davids exhaust themselves hurling their stones at giants. Usually they burn out and move to other careers. Barry W. Lynn would not burn out. From the 1970s to the 2010s he used his lawyer skills, his keen mind and devastating wit, and his pastoral empathy against the Goliaths. He aimed his smooth stones at those who would punish young people who refused to kill others in war (Book 1), at those who would withhold rights protected in the First Amendment of the U.S. Constitution (Book 2), and at the Religious Right that sought to erase the Constitution's core principle of the separation of church and state (Book 3).

His stones were his keen legal arguments and he delivered them with sharp humor. That made him a popular speaker at press conferences and hearings, on television and radio and podcasts. This is his story. It includes politicians and activists, as well as the comedians, musicians, actors, and movies that kept him sane as he persisted. Lynn's phenomenal ability to keep engaging in debate and conversation with leaders of those Goliaths, entering their spaces to listen to them and take them on, makes his story an entertaining and educational tour of the last five decades.

Blue Cedar Press

Chapter 1

WHY WRITE THIS BOOK?

My wife Joanne and I used to have many big parties, especially focusing on Halloween because a Halloween gathering in 1967 had been our first date. At one such party, the teenaged son of one of Joanne's co-workers came up to me and announced, "I want to do what you do."

Curious, I inquired, "And what do you think I do?"

His response, "You get paid to piss people off!"

It wasn't all that I did, but I did manage to tick off a lot of people.

This book is being written during the pandemic of 2020-2022 and would probably not have been written at all if this viral threat had not materialized. After all, how many walks in the nearby woods could I take? How many Grade Z movies could I stream? Instead, I decided to reflect on my career and again postpone learning to play the guitar, although I did take six virtual lessons from Maine singer-songwriter Caroline Cotter.

I've held three major jobs: post-Vietnam relief for war resisters and battles over draft registration at the United Church of Christ, anti-censorship efforts at the American Civil Liberties Union, and battling the theocratic goals of America's Religious Right as head of Americans United for Separation of Church and State. In all three, I have pissed people off. I've tried, not always successfully, to choose not to hate those whose beliefs I considered to be misguided, and I've maintained a sense of humor throughout.

One can measure her or his life in many ways: how many toys you have acquired, how much money is in your retirement account, how many people you have slept with. I wouldn't judge anyone for using these metrics. But lately, I find myself reviewing my life by recalling the extraordinary people I have run into along the path of my career. Many of these people are to be found in the pages of this book. Some you will recognize, such as President Bill Clinton, Ralph Nader, Oliver North, and even Lauren Bacall, but there are plenty of folks who are not exactly "household names" too, such as Vietnam War Army Veteran Weldon S. Merchant, comic writer David Feldman, and songwriter Bianca De Leon.

I start this tale with five vignettes about moments in my life that changed my perspective on the world or gave me opportunities I never expected to have. They include stories about a sideshow, a conservative thinker, a beautiful con artist, a minister, and an Attorney General of the United States.

Chapter 2

THE FIVE PEOPLE WHO MOLDED ME

The Sideshow: Mother Doesn't Always Know Best

I was born in Harrisburg, Pennsylvania, on July 20, 1948, and lived there until I was nearly five when the family moved to Bethlehem, Pennsylvania. An only child, born to parents who decided to have one child late in life, I recall many pleasant activities: sipping orange juice from a candy straw while sitting on the porch in a thunderstorm, reading Classics Illustrated comic books, and peering through the dusty window of an old garage that I firmly believed contained a decaying space alien.

Barry Lynn in a school photo, undated.

One of the biggest thrills of each year was attending the Greater Allentown State Fair. I loved fairs and carnivals with their rickety rides, nearly impossible to win games, and garish posters for all the attractions on the midway. One year, I almost met popular comedian Red Skelton because my father knew one of the fair's entertainment bookers. Unfortunately, as usual, we arrived too late for the informal pre-show "meet and greet." At that time—the late 1950s—many shows were unfortunately referred to as "freak shows," one for human freaks and one for animal freaks. I bugged my parents incessantly for a chance to see the human one—it was fifty cents, with an additional quarter to see the hermaphrodite. Really I was much too young to see said hermaphrodite and didn't even know what the word meant. My folks had absolutely no interest in seeing any of this and reluctantly gave me the money to go in by myself, warning me not to stay too long.

The Fifties were the heyday of the James E. Strates Shows, the best-known provider of carnival and fair midways on the East Coast. They were known for "exhibiting" folks such as Grace McDaniels, labeled "The Mule Faced Woman" because her face was severely deformed with purple tumors (a condition called Sturge-Weber Syndrome); Stanley Berent, the "Seal Boy" who had no hands and short arms described as "flippers"; and a number of people labeled as "pinheads," born with a condition called microencephaly and familiar to cinemaphiles who have seen director Todd Brownings' film *Freaks*. These were the kind of people in that tent, along with a magician who entertained between the "human oddities," the only slightly less offensive term occasionally used to replace "freaks."

For some inexplicable reason, when he asked for a volunteer that night in 1958, I raised my hand and got up on the stage with him. I had little to do, but the audience seemed to like it when I would hand him a prop, or he'd pull a quarter out of my ear. This was not exactly David Copperfield grade material, but I was thrilled to be a part of it. I could get people to like me just by going up on a stage!

After roughly forty-five minutes, my mother showed up at the back of the tent. I knew immediately that she didn't like what she was seeing. She motioned for me to come down, and I left with her. Once outside she asked me whether the foray was worth it, and I acknowledged that I was uncomfortable with the way the performers were treated, that some even seemed to be presented as objects of ridicule. My mother was a terribly nice person and she said, "Barry, they really should be glad to have a job there—who else would hire them?"

Much as I respected my mother's opinions, something about her response bothered me. It gradually dawned on me that the problem of their unemployability was much more the fault of the people who wouldn't hire them than with themselves. We marginalized such people, and we should not have. Years later, for example, I learned that Grace McDaniels had been married, was known as an incredible mother to her two children, embraced her disability, and had enormous self-respect.

So, that night, I learned two big lessons. I learned that I enjoyed being in the spotlight, despite my innate shyness. Second, and of far more significance, not marginalizing people who were living outside the mainstream became a kind of "moral imperative." Not having read Kant at the time, I am not even sure how I framed it, maybe it "just felt wrong."

Decades later, I was doing a daily radio show with ultra-conservative pundit and Nixon aide Pat Buchanan every weekday for about a year and a half, and he once asked me, "Why didn't you ever work for a President?" I joked that I had never found one who was moral enough. There was a bit of truth to that, but the main reason was that my interests were always focused on people who had no power, persons living on the fringes of the culture, and people whose opinions rankled those in power. My acquaintance Jim Hightower of Texas, who parlayed his election as the state Commissioner of Agriculture into a life of writing, radio hosting, and generally annoying people in power, was a champion of the dispossessed, saying, "The only thing you find in the middle of the road are yellow lines and dead skunks." I concur with him.

The Conservative Icon Who Turned Me into a Progressive

My father was a huge fan of William F. Buckley, Jr., conservative writer and creator of the magazine *National Review*, which has been perhaps the most influential conservative publication in America. Since I had enormous respect for my dad, I was also a fan. My father came home one fall evening in 1965 with the big news that Buckley was coming to Lehigh University in our hometown of Bethlehem to debate the founder of the Socialist Party, Norman Thomas. Of course, we sat in the basketball gymnasium to hear what I assumed would be Buckley's evisceration of Thomas—to be accomplished with the aplomb I knew Buckley was capable of, having seen him occasionally on television.

Thomas was quite frail by that time in his life and couldn't keep up with Buckley's wit. He had the strength of his convictions but barely the capacity to stand up. But as I sat there, I realized that his wisdom surpassed that of Buckley. The more Buckley pontificated about his agenda of ultra-individualism, the more I wondered how that could possibly mesh with the ideas I was learning as a devout Sunday School attendee. Where was his concern for the "least among us?" Where was the sense of shared community responsibility?

These ideas were absent from Buckley's worldview. His autonomous actors, who believed they needed no one but themselves, who thought they had bootstrapped themselves to the top as self-made souls, simply didn't seem to fit the model of true Christians. Buckley's human beings had nothing like a clear moral viewpoint and accepted no responsibility toward anyone else.

I can still remember sitting on the bleachers that night when the debate ended, unable to stand up, in a kind of moral paralysis from the nascent transformation of my values that had occurred over the past two hours. Thus began my utter rejection of political conservatism. Later in my life, I would have many encounters with Buckley.

Sitting in my office one day in 1982, I got a phone call from a man named Warren Steibel. He told me he was the producer of Buckley's popular PBS show *Firing Line* and that he had just received a fundraising letter from Americans United for Separation of Church and State (AU) with my signature on it. (Like every other non-profit, AU, which I led for twenty-five years, spent a small fortune soliciting for new members through a highly choreographed direct mail program—costly but successful). Warren said he wanted to do one of Buckley's two-hour specials on the Religious Right. He was curious if I'd like to join the anti-Religious Right side of a four-person team. I said yes.

As he continued to explain who he was, he noted that he was a liberal and that he had directed an obscure movie called *The Honeymoon Killers*. That film wasn't obscure to me, and I said, "I've seen that film twice, in the two places you should see it—at a drive-in and at the American Film Institute." He was quite impressed. I just hoped my debate performance would match my good taste in films.

That *Firing Line* episode, called, "Resolved: We Should Not Fear the Religious Right," was the first in a series that I did over the years. Defending the Religious Right were Buckley, Illinois Republican

Congressman and anti-abortion zealot Henry Hyde, the rarely seen (except on his own daily broadcast) Pat Robertson (founder of The Christian Broadcasting Network and Regent University, who had recently given up his ministerial standing to run for President), and Rabbi Jacob Nussbaum. Opposing the Right, I was joined by Ira Glasser (deliberately mispronounced by Robertson as "Glazer" to emphasize that he was Jewish), Harvard scholar Cornel West, and Harriet Woods, the first woman to hold statewide office in Missouri (as Attorney General). The event was held at the University of South Carolina.

I had a direct one-on-one questioning of Robertson, where, to demonstrate that there was good reason to fear the wackiness of his beliefs, I brought up his belief that only Christians and Jews should hold public office. "Would you like to have Muammar Quaddafi as Secretary of Defense?" he asked. I also questioned him about his idea that Jimmy Carter and George Bush were "carrying out the mission of a tightly knit cabal whose goal is a new world order for the human race under the domination of Lucifer," and again he responded that foreign military commanders should not lead American troops, a non-sequitur and a perfectly dopey non-response.

As the audience was leaving, I realized that, since Ira and Pat were both there, I should get a picture with my arms around them because I was the only person in history who, as I reminded them, "ever worked simultaneously for the ACLU and Pat Robertson." Pat looked slightly confused but then offered the observation, "That's right, you were on my radio network." Indeed, I used to leave my office at the ACLU late each afternoon and drive to a small radio station in Silver Spring, Maryland, to do a program called *Battleline*. I wish I could find that photograph.

These *Firing Line* debates were always moderated by Michael Kinsley, writer for *The New Republic*, *Slate*, and *Politico*, and long-time co-host of CNN's *Crossfire* with Pat Buchanan. Michael would often introduce me as the host of *Battleline*, and then note, "which sounds like a rip-off of both *Firing Line* and *Crossfire*." Kinsley was an extraordinarily bright and witty person who was slowed down dramatically with Parkinson's disease in 1992. He underwent deep brain stimulation to reduce its symptoms and, true to form, wrote an article for *Time* that concluded with what he claimed were his first words coming out of anesthesia, "Well, of course, when you cut taxes, government revenues go up. Why couldn't I see that before?"

My favorite of these specials dealt with evolution and was filmed at Seton Hall University in New Jersey. I was the "team captain" on that one, defending science and therefore evolution in a special titled, "Resolved: Evolutionists Should Accept Creation." I was joined by National Center for Science Education director, Dr. Eugenie Scott; head of Brown University's Biology Department, Dr. Kenneth Miller; and philosopher of science, Michael Ruse. We were up against Buckley, Lehigh University biology professor Michael Behe, mathematician David Berlinski, and historian Philip Johnson.

My favorite part of that show was my summation. I noted to the devout Berlinski, who had written that the Gospel of John was his favorite book of the Bible, "David, I share your love of the Gospel of John. It begins with the words: 'In the beginning was the Word' and, after tonight, I am more convinced than ever that that 'Word' was 'evolve.'"

Not only did that tick him off but I received an enormous volume of mail trying to correct my theology. Of course, the play on words got me a lot of laughs that night.

I did several more of these debates, always before a college audience and without any editing at all—Warren said, "If it happens, it's on the show." This was never clearer than during a debate entitled "Resolved: That the ACLU Is Full of Baloney." I did that one long after leaving the ACLU, but Warren wanted me back again. Nadine Strossen, a law professor and then Board President of the ACLU, was also on the show, along with Leon Botstein, the President of Bard College in Annandale-on-Hudson, the location of the debate.

One of Buckley's partners was Bill Donahue, who had written a book-length diatribe against the ACLU and was the head of the Catholic League for Individual Freedom—an organization that had no actual connection to the Catholic hierarchy but defended and excused all manner of Catholic excesses. He was joined by law professor at the University of Texas, Lino Gralia, and professional homophobe, who then worked at Concerned Women for America, Robert Knight. Donahue started off interrogating Nadine about the Florida ACLU affiliate's defense of "dwarf bowling."

16

When the President of Bard began to speak, women students started a demonstration in the back of the auditorium. He couldn't continue speaking. Warren was not going to turn off the cameras, but Nadine, a champion of free speech, went to the microphone, explained that disruptions were not free speech, and told the students that if they wanted to write up their demands, she was sure we would all be glad to give the students the opportunity to read their demands at the end of the show. That is exactly what they wanted to do and their dispute with the College is right there on the video of that debate. Their protest, however, didn't stop there.

College President Botstein was scheduled to have a debate with Gralia on the 14th Amendment a half hour after the *Firing Line* taping. The students announced that they would go on to disrupt that also. Warren asked if I would substitute for Botstein, since it was only a thirty-minute encounter.

I like the 14th Amendment and knew a few, very few, historical facts about it, so I agreed. It wasn't bad and provided more proof for me that if you sound like you know something and say it brazenly enough, you can probably get away with trading on the little you do know. I am proud to say that this was the only time I went into any debate without being over-prepared.

When Buckley decided to retire, he did a few of the thirty-minute versions of *Firing Line* in Washington, including one on the "success" of the American conservative movement, and asked me to debate with the Heritage Foundation's Lee Edwards, an extremely nice guy who was heralded as the principal historian of the American conservative movement. At one point, I just said bluntly, "I cannot think of a single good idea the conservative movement has ever had." Both Buckley and Edwards seemed incredulous, then mumbled a few things about tax cuts. Frankly I haven't seen anything in the decades following that made me change my mind.

Buckley was a most interesting debate opponent. My favorite recollection was a conversation I had with him on a small plane going to another taping in Columbia, South Carolina. As we chatted, I told him about that long ago encounter at Lehigh with Norman Thomas, "Bill, you lost me that night. So, please know: You actually created me."

Beauty and the Con

I had returned for my second year at Dickinson College where I did my undergraduate work after nearly deciding to transfer to Columbia University in New York City, imagining the cultural life would surpass the opportunities in Carlisle, Pennsylvania. As a member of the Debate Team, I had to sit as the recruiter at its table for an "activities night" for freshmen. Somehow, most of the people attracted to that table were not terribly interesting to me.

For some reason the table next to this one was vacant. I thought it might be fun to change that. I wrote up a note that said: "YOUNG ANARCHISTS CLUB! Because we do not believe in any hierarchy at all, we have no officers and no spokespersons, so there is no one here to talk with you. If you are interested in joining, however, sign up below." I added a few phony signatures and figured I'd see what happened.

And then she walked by. She was breathtakingly beautiful. Her name was Joanne, and she actually was interested in the debate team. I was certainly interested in her. Of course, in junior high school I had been interested in Ann Margret, too, and that didn't come to anything. One of her fellow incoming students stopped by the area and read the bogus recruitment form for the anarchists. He commented to Joanne that he had never heard of this club.

Then she said it.

"That is a really important activity. All the best people on campus are associated with it. You should sign up for more information." She even suggested he might want to sign up as the Club's President. What a con artist! He signed the paper. I smiled at her. I recall being otherwise speechless.

When I returned to my dorm room, I told John McClellan, one of my roommates, that I had just met the woman I was going to marry.

"Sure," he said, "sure."

I couldn't sleep. She had been so good at scamming that guy. And she was so damn pretty.

Had I gone to Columbia, my entire life would have been different. I had learned by listening to the opening lines of an episode of *The Outer Limits* television series that "If you change the position of a single pebble on a beach, you change the course of history." But I met Joanne. We were inseparable for the next three years.

I was dating someone before I met Joanne and she was scheduled to go to an ROTC Military Ball with a junior, but things changed quickly for both of us. Those other dating opportunities dissipated (some lying was involved), and we went on our first real date, at an off-campus Halloween party. Neither of us ever seriously dated anyone else again. An obscure rock group called the Sunshine Company was playing its "hits" like "Happy" and "Back on the Street Again" a few weeks after Halloween, and we were there; the brilliant Paul Butterfield Blues Band with Paul's iconic harmonica style came to campus a few weeks later, and we were there.

We became inveterate movie-goers in nearby Harrisburg. Joanne had only seen two films before she met me, *Gone with the Wind* and *Swiss Family Robinson,* so she had a great deal of catching up to do. We shared almost every lunch and dinner. Since I rarely got up for breakfast, being careful not to repeat my freshman year mistake of scheduling classes at eight in the morning even on Saturdays, Joanne often left a single serving box of cereal in my college mailbox.

We studied together, usually in a small room on the top floor of the library, so my grade point average went up. Indeed, by the time we graduated, she was #2 in class rank, only outdone by a Latin major and followed by me at #3. I had gotten a B in the required gym class, wherein I had explored the athletic activity of archery for one semester.

Our excursions also included going to protests against the Vietnam War and racial inequality locally and in New York City and Washington, DC, and driving to movies and concerts as far away as Baltimore and Philadelphia.

We also had to weather her father's absolute hatred of the idea of us getting married upon graduation. He threatened to pull her out of college—something even college President Howard Rubendall weighed in against, saying that this was a terrible idea. Her father initially refused to help pay her medical school tuition. Even as our wedding day approached, just a week after our graduation, he did not relent.

He was a prominent physician in Morgantown, West Virginia, and his friends gave us all kinds of expensive presents. As we were sitting on the floor of his living room looking over the stuff we had been given, he walked in and, noticing a silver shrimp dish, observed, "I guess you won't be using that, living in the Bowery." I had long before decided that I would not lose any more sleep over such comments. As it turned out, we never lived in the Bowery and never used the shrimp bowl anywhere we did live. Even at the wedding, at the back of the church before walking up the aisle, he said to Joanne, "You know you don't have to go through with this."

We recently celebrated our 50th wedding anniversary. To commemorate the fact that Joanne had disappeared for a half hour at our post-wedding dinner to watch the Belmont Stakes, the third jewel in the Triple Crown of horse racing, we always watch that race some way—in a sports bar, on our own television, once when in Europe over a YouTube video posted moments after the race. We had never seen it in person and would joke, "Let's go on our 50th anniversary." A few months before the race in 2020, we checked out the options to see it right there in New York. We got a fancy hotel, paid for parking close to the track and then splurged more on box seats complete with a buffet or two. Then COVID-19 came and the race and our trip to watch it were canceled.

In fact, June 6, 2020, turned out to be a very different day than expected. For the first time since the pandemic began, we went into Washington, for the DC version of Black Lives Matter demonstrations in the wake of the police killings that had occurred over the prior two weeks. We got a "take out" dinner and watched another event we had hoped to see live: "The Sexy Liberal Comedy Tour" featuring Stephanie Miller, comedian and daughter of Barry Goldwater's little-remembered running mate Bill Miller, along with my friend and radio host/actor/ comic John Fuegelsang and several other comedians and guest singer-songwriter Jill Sobule. That was a worthy set of experiences and so we say: "Let's see the Belmont live for our 53rd anniversary."

A Minister: The First Boss That Mattered

When Joanne was applying to medical school, she was actually asked on occasion why she felt she should take a slot from a deserving male student. She enrolled in the Boston University School of Medicine, which was not easy given the sexism in the medical world. I had decided to try to be admitted to a night law school program, which limited the search to Boston, Pittsburgh, or Washington, DC.

In 1974, Joanne began an internship at George Washington University Hospital and I started at night at Georgetown University Law Center. I had attended Boston University's School of Theology and had been ordained in the ministry in 1973. I could not believe my good fortune to find that the DC-based social action office of the United Church of Christ in the spring of 1974 was looking for an intern to run its To Heal a Nation program, looking to salve the pains of the post-Vietnam era. A principal objective was to achieve amnesty for the estimated tens of thousands of war resisters characterized as draft evaders or "deserters," depending on whether the man had or had not taken the oath of military service. This seemed ideal. I had known of this part of the United Church of Christ for years and always viewed working in that office as the pinnacle of career success.

BETHANY UNITED CHURCH OF CHRIST
Bethlehem, Pennsylvania

C. Lamar Derk, Pastor   Mrs. Glenn Koplin, Organist

THE ORDER OF SERVICE FOR THE ORDINATION OF
Barry W. Lynn

PRELUDE—"Toccata on Deo Gratias" ....Biggs

CALL TO WORSHIP

*PROCESSIONAL HYMN 15—"All Creatures of Our God and King"

    Minister: Christ is with us!

    PEOPLE: HE IS WITH US INDEED!

    Minister: In joy and contrition we come before God.

    PEOPLE: LET US CONFESS OUR SINS.

*CONFESSION OF SIN:

Barry Lynn is ordained in the ministry of the United Church of Christ in 1973

Since we were coming to Washington the very next week to look for housing, preferably in a less rat-infested neighborhood than we were about to leave in Boston, I called the person whose name was on the job announcement, the Reverend Paul L. Kittlaus. When I asked if I could come in to see him that Monday, Paul was courteous, but he said he didn't see much point in meeting me. He said they already had a perfect candidate, a young man from Minnesota who had resisted the draft himself and had served a brief stint in prison for having done so. Moreover, Paul had to leave mid-morning to catch a plane. Although not used to being this pushy, I told him I thought he'd be making a mistake not seeing me. All I wanted was fifteen minutes. He reluctantly acceded to the request. I felt that this denomination "owed" me fifteen minutes, so I was feeling a bit self-righteous knowing I had been granted it. I got together a sermon I had once preached on amnesty, my resume, and a few other articles and prepared to be as impressive as I could be.

In fact, I was petrified. Not only would this have to be a come-from-far-behind victory, but I only had fifteen minutes to make my case. Most people can't say "hello" in fifteen minutes. When I arrived at the building housing the UCC office, right across from the Supreme Court building, I noticed that there were wild strawberries in the grass outside. As a committed Bergmanphile (a fan of Ingmar Bergman films), I knew this was some kind of sign. Since one of Bergman's major cinematic themes is the "silence of God," how God sometimes fails to give you the answer no matter how many times you ask the question, the sign may just have been: Don't expect an answer. In this case, Bergman proved temporarily correct.

Clearly, interviewer Kittlaus was impressed by my background and tenacity. After a few more than the promised fifteen minutes, he said he would be "proud to have the United Church of Christ represented by me in the halls of Congress." But there was that big issue of the other candidate. Paul said he was interested in seeing if something could be worked out for both of us but didn't appear overly optimistic about it. I thought things had gone a far distance, however, and left his office with a sense that there was a good chance I'd hear something the next day when I got back to Boston. I was also impressed that he had a poster behind his desk by activist nun Sr.

Corita that read, "If Jesus Comes Again, He Better Come in the Form of a Loaf of Bread."

When the telephone rang the next afternoon around 4:00, it was Paul offering me the job in Washington, with the other candidate to pursue field work in the Midwest and come to Washington occasionally. I have never wanted a job more since that day; in many ways, Paul Kittlaus "created" me as a professional activist by finding a creative solution to what some would have seen as a relatively simple, insignificant personnel issue.

The Best Attorney General in America

But could this whole activism thing continue? During the mid-1970's movement to achieve a "universal, unconditional amnesty," I found myself very much in the center of those efforts. In 1974, I was at a fundraising event in the Upper West Side of New York. The main attraction was Ramsey Clark, the Attorney General in President Lyndon Baines Johnson's administration. Clark had become a vigorous opponent of the Vietnam War and thought it essential that relief be given to those who refused to participate in that conflict.

Before he spoke, he introduced me, mentioned that we had done some press conferences together, and then asked me to say a few words. When I finished, he noted: "I believe this young man has signed on for the long haul to justice." I was moved by this, and it was one sentence I always remembered when I considered taking a job outside of the world of social justice. Any such position would have made Ramsey Clark a liar and I couldn't countenance that.

So, my mother focused my attention, Buckley changed my ideology, Joanne gave me a person to share life with, Paul gave me a chance to start a lifetime of activism in pursuing social justice, and Ramsey Clark made sure that activism would continue. I'll speak about some of these people more in the pages that follow. But looking back at my life from age seventy-four, these five people made all the difference in my world.

I did want this book to be a vehicle for thanking the hundreds of people who have made my life so engaging and satisfying. Most of them are people I love and respect, but a few are genuinely horrible human beings from whom I learned how not to engage with others.

As a child growing up, there were many things I expected to do: getting married (possibly to an Italian woman), fathering at least one child, and settling down as a pastor in a moderate sized town like Bethlehem, Pennsylvania.

Here's what happened. I got married (to a woman from West Virginia), had two great children, and went on a roller-coaster ride I never imagined taking. Growing up, I never envisioned being on *The Phil Donahue Show* or appearing regularly on network news, being the "Quote of the Day" in *The New York Times* on multiple occasions, speaking to a million people for two minutes on the National Mall, or getting to know any world-class musicians, comedians, and actors. Nor did I anticipate having two clergymen pray for my death or coming just moments from dying only a few weeks after retiring (something I don't attribute to those imprecatory prayers).

This book is about what that life, so far, has been, with some lessons learned, some reflections on people I've met (the good, the bad, and the ugly), and a lot of stories from my life and career.

This would not have been written except for the calamity that was (and continues to be) COVID-19 and the reshaped lives it has brought. I would have continued to read books, but probably would not have written much, since I'd go to at least three movies each week, often driving an hour to get to my favorite theaters; and I'd travel to countries I'd long hoped to visit. COVID-19 shutdowns changed all that.

Chapter 3

MY EARLY LIFE

Edith and Harold Lynn: My Parents

I'll admit that I sometimes stop reading autobiographies or memoirs when too many chapters cover generations that precede the author. My paternal grandfather raised racing pigeons on his roof. My maternal grandmother was transfixed by the television coverage of the coronation of Queen Elizabeth while I found it excruciatingly boring. Enough about them, only my own parents had any real impact on my life. I will start there.

Parents often set patterns for their children. My mother tried—she lived a lifetime of routine and hoped I would keep living it too. She met my father while she was working as a secretary at the Bethlehem Steel Company when Dad was a salesman there. I came along about a year after their marriage, and she never worked outside the home again.

Every afternoon she cooked a big dinner, except on those rare occasions when there was a planned outing to Walp's Restaurant, a Pennsylvania Dutch cookery in nearby Allentown, or to the Fireside Grill, serving the best cheeseburgers in America, then or now (Five Guys included), and just a short drive from our two-bedroom house on Eighth Avenue across from the ramp from the major highway through town. Her in-home cooking unfailingly contained meat, potatoes, two vegetables (tending to be of different colors), and a huge dessert.

My mother never acquired some skills, including driving a car. She blamed me for that. She claimed I laughed at her efforts while sitting in the back seat of our Buick. I always thought she had a more deep-seated distrust of automobiles, but it was years before she told me about two car-related calamities that undoubtedly sullied her enthusiasm. As a teenager in the 1920s, she was regularly dating a man at the same time he was dating another young woman. She'd been his date on a Friday; her competition was out on Saturday. On that night, he drove into a poorly marked parking garage in Allentown, Pennsylvania. With no markings for an open elevator shaft, he drove into it and the two of them were killed. This tragedy also explained her deep-seated fear of riding in elevators. Her own father was killed in an accident when the crank used to start his Model-T whipped back and broke his arm. Without antibiotics it became so infected that he died.

My dad was a great father, and I tended to believe everything he said. He was thin and not much interested in exercise, and indeed was ironically nicknamed "Muscles" when he was in college at Lehigh University (proof evidenced by his entry in the college yearbook). This meant he didn't push me to play much baseball or do other physical things I was uninterested in pursuing.

He was a wonderful teacher, though. One of my earliest recollections is sitting in an ice cream store in Bethlehem and having him explain the value of coins. I was inclined to think the size of a coin was commensurate with its value: a quarter was worth more than a dime, so I naturally thought a nickel was worth more than a dime, too. He straightened me out. He helped me develop a fondness for reading, took me to Sunday School at the Bethany Evangelical and Reformed Church, and answered all my questions during the Big Talk.

On the routine front, we always went to the same two places on summer vacation. My dad only got three weeks of time off—one was Christmas week; one was spent at the Hotel Lincoln in Ocean City, New Jersey; and the third was to a shifting venue at one of several resorts in the Pocono Mountains.

Ocean City was a kind of beach compromise between the overbuilt Atlantic City (with its Steel Pier and its famous diving horse) in its pre-casino days and the too-frenetic pace of Wildwood. This city had some amusements, lots of "penny arcades," five miniature golf courses (we played every morning), and four on-the-boardwalk movie theaters. The most remote, the "Surf," often showed horror movie double features. I recall the thrill of seeing that *The Deadly Mantis* was listed on a poster on the way into town, particularly knowing that my parents had already agreed to take me to any movie of my choice that year. There was the annual Sunday night arrival quick trip to the Boardwalk for some Kohr Brothers custard. Every year I got it in a cone, not a cup, and every year it melted onto my "good pants." Every year! Every night we had dinner at the Hotel Lincoln dining room—I never varied my order from turkey, mashed potatoes and jellied cranberry sauce. Never. Lunch was also always the same, eaten precisely one hour before going to the beach for a swim: one cheeseburger, French fries, and a vanilla milkshake.

My mother had a temper I rarely saw, although it was memorable when it erupted. It was usually preceded by the question, "Do you want to give me a heart attack?" She put up with all kinds of activities of mine, including making gunpowder. Making it requires only charcoal, sulfur, and saltpeter. The first two were in my Gilbert's chemistry set and the third was on the shelf at Yohe's Pharmacy, a few blocks from our house. When the pharmacist started wondering why a twelve-year-old needed to buy saltpeter every week, I had to ride my bike to more remote neighborhoods to get it. My friends and I used our homemade gunpowder to shoot off "rockets" in the backyard. She wasn't upset, because the Pennsylvania state trooper who was one of our neighbors thought it was harmless fun. We did too, until a classmate, experimenting with the same components, put his makeshift "bomb" in a vice in his basement, pounded on the item, and lost one of his eyes from the ensuing explosion.

Mom put up with even my oddest friends, watched us make 8mm movie versions of stories from *Classics Illustrated* comics, and was constantly urging me to spend more time "outside." During an outside filming of *The Oregon Trail*, one of my fellow actors dropped a wooden rifle on my head and I still have a scar above my left eye to prove it.

She was deeply in love with my dad, Harold. A decade after he died, she told me, "I was never really happy again." Dad had had an operation a decade before his death and was wheeled to the operating room without Mom having a chance to say anything to him. Dad made it through the surgery, but seeing her in that hospital fearful that he might not survive was one of the saddest things I ever witnessed. Years later, with the help of one of my favorite pastors, the Rev. Donald Esslinger, I performed the funeral service for my dad, and she and I could barely contain the tears, particularly when we played one of their favorite songs from Broadway's *The Music Man*.

My dad, too, had his routines. We ate at six o'clock every night, precisely forty minutes after he got back from work at Bethlehem Steel, forty-five if he stopped at the candy store for gummy orange slices. Dinner followed one glass of sherry and a quick read of that largely forgotten creation, the afternoon newspaper, *The Bethlehem Globe Times*. Those afternoon papers were important in that pre-internet era. This was printed so late that on November 22, 1962, the headline screamed "PRESIDENT IS SLAIN" with the edition a mere half-hour late in arriving. Kennedy had been assassinated at 12:30 p.m., Central Time.

The news became incredibly important to me. At some point in high school, I stopped eating dinner with my parents so I could sit in our living room and watch the local news from Philadelphia's Channel 6 (home to Chief Halftown and my first crush, "cowgirl" Sally Starr). I was convinced this aided my digestion; apparently so were my parents. After dinner, I could talk with them for hours, but just not over the pot roast.

My dad was very much a product of the Depression. He had studied chemical engineering at Lehigh University, but upon graduation, that field had no work. For years he subsisted on the wages paid by the Just Born Candy Company, now best known worldwide for gooey marshmallow Peeps. Then, it was beginning to market iconic candies for movie goers like Mike and Ike and Hot Tamales. Also on the creative docket was a black licorice concoction known unofficially during the 1920s in the nation's many penny candy stores as Nigger Babies.

He was instructed to put all the dirt from the floor into the vats of licorice, the black coloring covering that debris and giving a little bulk to the candy as a collateral benefit. He never ate licorice after the first night of his sweeping—and urged me unsuccessfully to do likewise. This confectionary product, sadly, was just one of the candies that played on repugnant racial stereotypes. Others were Picaninny Freeze (strawberry ice cream dotted with chocolate "seeds" advertised with a caricature of a young black girl with oversized red lips chomping on a slice of watermelon with the slogan: "Eat, seeds 'n all.") and Niggers' Toes advertised by a cowboy in blackface whose feet were Brazil nuts dipped in chocolate.

During the Depression, Dad also used his considerable piano playing skills to provide the music for silent movies. One of the last things he could do as he slumped into severe Parkinson's Disease was to play the background music for Charlie Chaplin and Harold Lloyd comedies and the rousing "Chariot Race March" from Ben Hur. One of the remaining pianists who still plays music from this silent era is Ben Model. I saw him perform in front of an obscure Harold Lloyd film at the American Film Institute in Silver Spring, Maryland, as I was finishing this manuscript.

My father eventually got a job with the social service agency in Pennsylvania, where he would deliver welfare checks to an array of colorful characters. These included a man who, owning no dishes, ate his meals from the lid of a large can of lard; a fellow who lived in a cave; and a third angry man who periodically threatened my father with the machete that he always kept with him.

When Dad finally got a sales job at Bethlehem Steel, he sold stone and slag, the latter a byproduct of the steel-making process often used in road construction. In the mid-Fifties he applied for a promotion there but did not get it and was thereby relegated to staying in that earlier position for over twenty years. He taught Sunday School, and some of his writings I found after his death were so theologically conservative that he did not accept the evidence for evolution. He was also the longtime secretary of The Cat and Dog Club, a small-time stock trading club where a group of men got together to pool funds to buy cheap speculative stocks. I was impressed that, before its bankruptcy, he was a shareholder in the Pickled Crow Gold Mine. However, I was even more impressed that he could make such witty comments about the previous month's gathering. I never forgot that use of humor in my subsequent life of speechmaking and column writing.

Like my mother, he had a rarely expressed temper. We had real disagreements over the Vietnam War, but the single biggest verbal explosion was over my planned trip to New York City on New Year's Eve in 1968 to hear a lecture by Dr. Timothy Leary about the use of LSD. Leary was the Sixties' greatest advocate for the use of hallucinogenic drugs like LSD and had been arrested on various drug charges since 1966. I had planned to drive there with a few friends in my own car (a clunker purchased from summer job money), but the weather was cold and snowy, and Dad absolutely refused to allow me to go. I didn't storm out, get in the car, and pick up my friends. I never used LSD either. Instead, I sat seething at home and watched the Times Square ball fall during a New Year's Eve show hosted by Dick Clark.

Dad became increasingly disabled with Parkinson's Disease after his retirement. The two institutions that he cherished the most during his life abandoned him. The church sent few visitors and then for only short visits. The Republican Party got into issues like abortion, which he thought was a personal moral matter about which politicians shouldn't have opinions that they wanted to turn into laws.

We moved my parents into our home in Virginia when my mother could no longer deal with his increasing disability. He could no longer walk or talk clearly. He had one brief five-minute period of clear speech when he looked out at our long driveway and thought (erroneously) that there were people standing at the end of it. Sometimes patients with Parkinson's have a brief period of consciousness known as "an awakening," which was the subject of a film with Robin Williams.

When I mentioned this film to movie critic/conservative political pundit Michael Medved during one of our frequent debates, he ridiculed the film. All I could think of was the incredible pleasure of having my father back for just a few moments. Forever after, I considered Medved to be lacking empathy. My dad also sat at our piano one day where he usually could just bang out some garbled notes—and suddenly he could play his old silent movie music clearly, for just a few minutes. It was wonderful, brief, and never repeated.

I never had any doubts about the love my parents had for me. I did have some resistance to their seeming enslavement to routines. Perhaps that was why I was willing to take risks in seeking jobs and was willing to live with ambiguity in daily life.

Kindergarten to High School

If all of my education had gone as poorly as my year in kindergarten at Calypso Elementary School in Bethlehem, I might be writing this memoir from a jail cell. My teacher was Mrs. Dornblatt, and she seemed to me an easy-to-anger, mean-spirited educator. My father heard my tales about her and developed a series of stories for me that featured an unpleasant character called Mrs. Darn Cat. Although I didn't know what satire was at the time, I did recognize that "punching up" (didn't know what that phrase meant either) was a useful way to handle people in power that you didn't care for.

My first-grade teacher, Miss Meehan, was everything her pedagogical predecessor was not: caring, supportive of students' efforts, and a big booster of reading. I recall reading a book featuring the characters of Alice, Jerry, and Jip (a canine) to my father as we were driving around town. Reading was thrilling. Fine, kind teachers throughout my elementary school career inspired me to get good grades, and I felt fully prepared to attend Nitschmann Junior High School for grades 7-9—it was right across the street from our house—and Liberty High School for grades 10-12 across town. The only flaw in those years was being put into an advanced math class in eighth grade that was incredibly difficult. My dad decided to intervene, correctly believing that I could learn pre-algebra anytime, and freed me from mathematical hell. I got moved to a regular class which had almost all female students and gave me a more manageable math class and friendlier teachers in the bargain.

I joined many clubs in high school: the debate team ("Resolved: Boxing Should Be Banned" was our first topic); Model United Nations (where I represented Libya twice but failed both times to get passed my proposed resolution to extend the scope of the twelve-mile limit for national waters); the Key Club (an invitation-only service club sponsored by the Kiwanis Club but sounded like the "key clubs" sponsored by Playboy magazine that were getting lots of publicity at the time); the National Honor Society; the band and orchestra. This joining frenzy was aimed at beefing up my college applications hoping that admissions committees would not notice my lack of athletic involvement. I was most interested in going to either the University of Pennsylvania in Philadelphia or Dickinson College in central Pennsylvania. Dickinson's College Bowl team had just won the championship during my last year of high school. When I got offered early admission to Dickinson, I took it immediately.

I graduated high school with 1,100 other students, among the largest graduating class in Pennsylvania. I was offered the chance to run for one of the two class speaker positions for graduation. About twenty-five of us had the chance to give a brief comment to our fellow classmates. If you got at least fifty supporters, as shown by the number of people who stood up when your comment was made, then you could try a five-minute address a week later. Five of us made it to that round. I came in second to a popular majorette. The two of us were on the program along with two other seniors selected by the faculty. One faculty member told *The Bethlehem Globe Times* after the elections, "If the students hadn't picked Barry, we would have." Thus I learned that one could appeal to the masses and the elites. It also gave me confidence to ask the popular Nancy Wachter to the senior prom. She accepted. After the prom, I don't think we ever went out again.

I had to memorize my speech for graduation night, which troubled me because I cannot to this day memorize much of anything.

There were many practice sessions, and a teacher positioned just off the stage prompted any of us who might forget the lines we had written. Much as I appreciated being selected, I was nervous about the event, nervous enough to throw up after my mother insisted that I eat dinner to "keep up my strength." I didn't need the prompter and the speech went over well. Somehow, I was able to sneak past the censors and include a veiled reference to the Vietnam War. I commented that a wise man had once said, "A mind is like a parachute; it only works when it is open." It was the last time I memorized a speech. Even at the time, memorizing your own words seemed odd, leaving no room for improvisation. That may have been the point.

olume XXV, No. 10   Liberty High School, Bethlehem, Pa.   March 18, 1966

Senior Class, Faculty Choose Four Speakers As Representatives At Commencement

Members of the school faculty and the senior class itsel were faced with a dilemma Tuesday, March 8. It seemec that neither party was able to limit its selection for clas: speaker to one person.

It was moved that the faculty and senior student body each choose two speakers. The individual speeches woulc then be shortened, the motion was seconded and passec with a vote of 551-315.

The two choices of the faculty are Candace Whitmer anc Jeffrey Bowker. Barry Lynn and Beverly Donchez are the _____ _ .. . . . .

Barry Lynn's graduation speech at Liberty High School, Bethlehem, PA (March 18, 1966).

A tape of that speech may exist in the school archives because the class had, for some inexplicable reason, agreed with Foster Forrest Frable, III, one of the most bullied students in the class, that our class gift should be a weird invention called a videotape machine. Now, both Liberty High School and the Ed Sullivan Show would have one. On that June night in 1966, the novel machine recorded our lengthy perambulations.

Haunted by Vietnam

People younger than me have a hard time comprehending the shadow that the war in Vietnam cast on young men in the Sixties and early Seventies. Ironically, even during the war, many Americans did not know how to pronounce the name of the country we were allegedly fighting to save, and probably most could not find it on a map.

America had "advisors" in Vietnam since the late Fifties. The first American casualties of the Vietnam Era (never declared a "war") were two young soldiers shot when one turned on the lights in a barracks to thread a new reel of film in a projector to continue the evening's entertainment. That was 1959.

I first became aware of Vietnam at the Hotel Lincoln, the destination of our yearly seaside summer vacation. The hotel had a large activities room for game nights, bingo, and movies. In 1963, we saw a 1957 film called *China Gate* which starred Gene Barry, Angie Dickinson, and singer Nat King Cole. The film focused on French involvement in Vietnam as they tried to eliminate the Communist influence of the Viet Minh. It was slightly critical of the French and was not shown in France for many years.

The next year, 1964, we were again in the Hotel Lincoln activity room watching the debate in the U.S. Senate on August 7 over what came to be known as the Gulf of Tonkin Resolution. This Senate declaration gave virtually unlimited authority to President Johnson to take "all necessary measures to repel any armed attacks against the forces of the United States and to prevent further aggression" by the Communist government of North Vietnam. The Resolution was based on claims, since debunked, that two Navy destroyers had been attacked by North Vietnam patrol boats. The House approved the Resolution unanimously, and in the Senate only Senators Wayne Morse of Oregon and Ernest Gruening of Alaska voted against it. Watching the debate, I assumed that the Resolution was justified and mentioned my concern over fighting a war there to my father. He responded: "This thing will all be over soon." It was not over until 1975, eleven years later, the longest U.S. war until Afghanistan and Iraq.

By 1965, one year later, I had become skeptical of the claims that the United States was playing any positive role in Vietnam. I had started to read critics of the war like Robert Scheer, editor of *Ramparts* magazine, and others who made a persuasive case that the U.S. had played a decisive role in preventing elections in Vietnam that almost certainly would have chosen Communist Ho Chi Minh to lead the reunited Vietnam.

By the fall of 1965, the U.S. military "action" was not over and was controversial enough to come up in a government class. As usual, I had an opinion, but now one shaped by my recent repudiation of conservative politics and my discovery that public speaking could be fun. This war was a mistake. It was intervention in a civil war. We should have just let a united Vietnam vote for a presidential candidate after the French had been thrown out of the country. The fact that the winner would certainly have been Ho Chi Minh was irrelevant. Democracy worked that way.

In the class of about thirty, no one agreed with my sentiments. At lunch, some guy I barely knew said, "You're the guy that's afraid to go to Vietnam to fight." I remember telling him that he was, in part, right.

At that time, I didn't even know there was an anti-war movement. I did see an occasional protester on television, usually CBS, which was my go-to network. However, when our band director, Ron Sherry, announced that my Liberty High School band would be performing at a Victory in Vietnam parade to support the troops, I asked him if attendance was required. When he said, "No," I was a little sorry he didn't want to argue with me. Maybe he wasn't all that political; maybe he just figured he and the listening audience could do without one second-string clarinet player. Nevertheless, not showing up felt good.

I'm not sure I knew then what a conscientious objector was, but I did know that going to college would give me a deferment, and that was good enough for the time being. I wrote a letter to the Lehigh Valley chapter of the ACLU commending them for their position that war in Vietnam was illegitimate.

On To College—Summer Jobs

Before I went to college, I decided to try a stretch as a door-to-door cutlery salesman. The high point of those eight weeks was being listed in *The Blade,* the Cutco Cutlery weekly publication which listed outstanding young knife sellers who hit some magic sales figure, probably $1,000 in a week. Even though the newsletter only reached a few hundred people, it was the first time my name had been in print outside of *The Bethlehem Globe-Times*. It was nearly miraculous that I sold any of these products.

The pitch was to walk up to the door and ask whoever answered, "I'm from Alcoa Aluminum. I'd like to show you a new product. All I need is a penny, a slice of bread, and an old kitchen knife. Can I come in?" This was really a breathtakingly idiotic approach. In addition, a few weeks after I started the job, eight Chicago nurses were killed by a knife-wielding psychopath named Richard Speck. Cutco did not change their approach. Perhaps no one in the company read the newspapers. Potential customers apparently did, making entrée even more difficult.

On those occasions when I did get inside and got the specified items brought to me by the occupants, I would complete my pitch on the veritably wonder-working power of my kitchen implements. I would demonstrate that the occupant's kitchen shears could not cut the penny, but my carbon steel ones would. Their old knife probably had a blade that was pulling away from a wooden handle. More significantly, that knife could not cut a slice of Wonder Bread lengthwise twice, thus preventing creation of thinly sliced finger sandwiches, a must-have skill for every homemaker. My knives could. Unfortunately, in my very first demonstration, I managed to cut my finger open as I tried the second slicing. I actually uttered the words, while declining a Band-Aid, "If I had cut myself with your old knife, I'd be worried about this." I bid a hasty retreat, recognizing failure, even at that tender period of youthful exuberance.

I was nearly prepared to abandon the whole knife and fork industry when Alice Raish, my neighbor, came to my rescue. She worked at the Allentown, Pennsylvania, newspaper, *The Morning Call,* preparing wedding and engagement announcements. She volunteered to give me the names and addresses of all the young women whose engagements were to be listed the next day. This goldmine permitted me a full day's advantage in pursuit of the single most likely candidate for purchasing about $144 worth of knives, kitchen shears, and other kitchen implements: the woman building a "hope chest." This period in America had lengthy engagements and men, who did not cook and therefore owned no cutlery or pots and pans, hoped their beloved spouses would have snapped up a decent set of each. After making a few thousand dollars on commissions, I sold my sample kit to my mother and spent the rest of the summer going to amusement parks and the movies.

The next two summers were spent at a patronage job for the Pennsylvania Department of Highways. I didn't know anything about local politicians, and I nearly didn't get the job the first year when I couldn't remember who the local Congressman was at the job interview conducted by the Bethlehem equivalent of a New York City ward boss (the Congressman was Democrat Fred Rooney). This was a job in name only. My principal duties were to show up, sign in, sit around outside or, in the case of rain, in my car, and observe excavation for sewer pipes, then wrap up the day by filling in a sheet of paper which indicated how much pipe had been laid. This was, of course, a two-man job. Someone had to hold one end of the measuring tape while the more experienced worker held the other and jotted down the measurement in a logbook.

The summer employees were college students who shared my incredulity at being paid for such a minimalist work product. One of my co-workers was a Haverford College philosophy major who was both a Marxist and an atheist. He talked about how the Hegelian dialectic ended, but the Marxist one continued. I tried to ignore him, and failing that, talked about Marx Brothers movies to try to convince him I thought Karl was one of them. Perhaps he came before Gummo.

Watching the long-term employees truly frightened me. I could not imagine working like this for a lifetime. One fellow was a severe alcoholic with whom one would never want to risk a drive for lunch, even if he was paying. Another was a man who could speak of nothing but "the change," an utterly incomprehensible transformation his wife had recently undergone which made him as bitter as he claimed she was. He suggested that I prepare myself for this event in the future of every man and do so promptly. He actually said it was something they wouldn't teach in college. The only young regular employee was a would-be police officer who shared with everyone his vivid sexual fantasies about what he would convince women to do to him to avoid the speeding tickets he would someday be empowered to hand out.

In two summers, there was only one event which made me feel that I had done anything useful. My Marxist co-worker and I were sent out to observe a blacktop paving project and, of course, to measure the amount paved at the end of each day. The blacktop was supposed to be laid over a fairly firm bed of rock. One morning, the crew decided to dump an enormous tree trunk into the road excavation, thus filling up a huge space that would not require those expensive rocks. We discussed the obvious illegality of this maneuver, and the near-certainty that the trunk would quickly rot, creating a giant pothole that a school bus filled with young children would pass over. This dangerous possibility needed to be corrected, and we went to the job foreman to demand the trunk's extraction. I thought there was a good chance he would kill and bury us, thus saving a few more feet of rock. Instead, he did some perfunctory grousing and hauled the tree to the side of the road. To this day, no school bus has crashed on that stretch of Pennsylvania highway.

The lesson from these summers was that whatever work I eventually did would have to have some connection to a higher purpose than avoiding my future wife's menopause or obtaining some free sex along the side of the road.

Dickinson College

It was my father who drove me to college. My mother was too emotional to go along. I knew that my roommate was to be Horace Lincoln Jacobs IV from Florida, who was trying out for the football team and thus had arrived a week earlier. I didn't actually meet him until close to midnight because he was out at a party. He seemed a nice enough person and right before we went to sleep that night he said: "This is a very tough school. Lots of incoming students never graduate." This warning increased my level of nervousness. It led me to study a lot. "Linc," as he preferred to be called, took another route: bought his textbooks at the school store, put them in a shopping bag, and never removed them. I believe his grade point average for that first semester was 0.2, which meant that he failed all classes except the one in which he received a "D." When he left Dickinson, I was assigned a new roommate, another Floridian named Paul Hanna.

Paul was a more studious roommate, but he had one incredibly annoying habit. He would tell me how much he needed to get up early for his morning classes and would set his very loud alarm clock. When the clock went off and woke me up, Paul slept on. After a few weeks of this, fed up with his promises to wake up, I took direct action. If the prongs of an electrical device are taped with adhesive tape and the device replugged into a wall socket, the device will not work. Paul found his alarm clock not moving so he just gave up trying to use it. He never examined the prongs. After leaving Dickinson at the end of his freshman year he became a successful bank officer where, presumably, he did not have to worry about the mechanism that kept the bank vault closed.

I was eager to fit in at Dickinson and thought about "pledging" to the one fraternity that seemed to cater to studious students like myself, Theta Chi. Many members of the debate team had joined, along with many of the student disc jockeys at the campus radio station. During my third visit to the fraternity house, though, a Debate Team member pulled me aside and said I had been "blackballed" by someone in the fraternity and would not be offered a slot in the pledge class. This hurt, but, frankly, I would probably have blackballed myself at that point since I was a geeky scholar who didn't fit in particularly well.

Interested in the camaraderie that fraternity life gave you, at least theoretically, I was excited to learn that some members of the campus "fringe," politically engaged predecessors to the Hippies, were trying to set up a new fraternity, Gamma Phi Epsilon. It was supposed to become an affiliate of Alpha Phi Epsilon after a year. Gamma Phi had fraternity pins and an off-campus apartment above a pizza shop right off the campus grounds. It lasted all of the time I was at Dickinson and recruited a few new pledges each year but never really became a serious activity on campus.

I had a few dates that first year with women I met at the campus church. The biggest draw at the church was not the theological acumen of the sermons but the invitations to lunches after the service. The college cafeteria served decent food, but it couldn't compete with the homemade lunches for us churchgoers. When the dating scene at church dissipated, I took to computer dating at nearby colleges, particularly at Wilson College, a few miles away. Each interested person filled out a questionnaire which went into a computer program that would match you with others with like minds. Buses would actually bring students who were matched with us to the campus for dates. The people I was matched with made me skeptical of computers for years; those matched with me probably had the same thought.

During that first year, I had many late-night snacks with other students who were getting bored by Dickinson. Although we could bring cars to campus the following year and would thus be able to visit the exciting city of Harrisburg for a broader range of cultural activities, I decided to leave and go to Columbia University in New York City, which had accepted me as a transfer student. I later revised this decision and stayed at Dickinson.

Despite my interest in transferring, Dickinson was an astonishingly good experience for me. I did have trouble, though, selecting a major. My faculty adviser insisted that I choose one or be thrown out of the college. I chose English. This forced me to read a lot of contemporaries of Shakespeare. I wrote my Shakespeare seminar paper on *Coriolanus*, one of the bard's lesser-known tragedies. Upon discovering that the paper was a few pages short of the required length and needing a quick early morning fix before the deadline, I went to the library as soon as it opened, found a book of all the ribald lines in Shakespeare, and composed a poem (doggerel actually) that consisted of one line for each letter of the alphabet.

What I gained most from the Dickinson experience, aside from meeting Joanne, were friendships that remain to this day and a love for multiple discipline learning, that thrill that came when the lessons from a psychology class melded with those from a history class, when a novel in English related to a non-Christian passage of scripture in my religious studies class.

How I Didn't Go to Vietnam

By the end of my freshman college year in the spring of 1967, I had located a number of other earnest opponents of the war and was able to convince the only one of us with a car to drive us to the big anti-war rally in New York City. Four hours up; four hours back, including taking a wrong turn in Delaware–it felt worth it. Tens of thousands of people, mostly young, were birthing a movement that would gradually change the shape of American politics. Don't let anyone tell you otherwise. I was in on it throughout college.

As my final year at college was winding down, I knew a few things. I was getting married the week after graduation. I had originally planned to go to law school but with my strong opposition to the Vietnam War, I was disappointed that major legal organizations like the American Bar Association were largely silent on the legality of the conflict. On the other hand, powerful voices in the clergy, including my fellow United Church of Christ clergyman William Sloane Coffin, as well as the Reverend Doctor Martin Luther King, Jr., were in the vanguard of those opposing the war on moral and legal grounds. This had led me to reconsider my future education. It also created a moral dilemma.

At that time in the history of the Selective Service System, there were a raft of complex exemptions and deferments. Going to graduate school was no longer an automatic deferment, but going to theology school was. I had a draft lottery number in the middle of the draw, but I couldn't justify getting a deferment based solely on my intention to become a member of the clergy.

I went to my Army pre-induction physical after a sleepless night, kept awake by the deep anger I felt about the war and the fundamentally evil people promoting and prolonging it. Potential draftees went to the pre-induction test center on a bus. I wore a denim work shirt with an armband on my left arm with red dye symbolizing blood. When asked to fill out a form regarding my background, I did not claim to be a conscientious objector. To get C.O. status one had to oppose war "in any form." I noted that I opposed the military draft based on the Ninth Amendment, although at the time, I did not even know what it said. Neither did the sergeant. When he asked if my armband was for a "medical reason," I said, "No, it is a political statement because I don't believe in bombing children." He didn't seem amused. In a final section on known medical history, I added that I had trouble sleeping.

The next stop was assessments by several physicians of my fitness for military service. The first doctor listened to my heart, shook his head, and asked if I knew I had a serious heart murmur. I did not. He said it would render me permanently ineligible to be in the military service and get me classified as 4-F. I asked what I should do about this, and he said, "Just watch it because there is nothing we can do to fix it." When I saw the psychiatrist who wanted me to describe my inability to sleep, I asked, "Well, doesn't everybody have that problem sometimes?"

When we all got together some hours later, a few who had low lottery numbers and had passed the physicals were directed to another room to be processed as 1-A. Not one of them looked proud or happy to be a part of that group.

When I got back to Carlisle and saw Joanne, I told her about the day's experiences and asked her about that "heart murmur." She was the librarian for the Biology Department and had easy access to a huge array of medical literature. Apparently, she discovered that this was a serious condition and that I would be lucky to survive until forty. She encouraged me to get yearly heart exams. Over time the intensity and nature of the murmur waxed and waned. Eventually, many years past forty, it got bad enough that I planned to have an operation the summer following my retirement. Life had other plans.

Bear Mountain Summers

Desperation can lead to many things, including snake handling. For me, snake handling had nothing to do with religious rituals. It came one Sunday in the form of huge but harmless snakes in a garbage can.

Joanne and I knew that, after a brief honeymoon, we needed jobs for the summer before heading on to graduate school in Boston. We saw a job description on a college bulletin board for couples to run nature museums in Bear Mountain State Park north of New York City. We wanted this job, despite my lack of experience with or knowledge of flora or fauna. I did possess a butterfly net as a child, but the idea of capturing these beautiful creatures and then pinning them in a box lost its appeal very quickly. Joanne, on the other hand, had grown up on a farm in West Virginia and knew how to take care of animals like horses and goats.

Our letter of application emphasized her background and our newlywed status. The only thing barely relevant to this job in my background was running a recreation center in one of the poorer sections of Bethlehem where my major task was to prevent kids from beating each other, or me, over the head with hockey sticks. I had accomplished this mainly by appealing to their burgeoning self-interest (as in, "If you hit John, his big brother will come out here one night and smack the shit out of you"). One older fellow used to come by to shoot baskets. Once I beat him in a game of Around the World and he became a friend. He was later arrested for attempted murder. I was glad to be his friend.

During that summer I reconnected with Coach Daniel Sylvester, who was my scary high school physical education teacher . He was, however, not as scary as his African American successor, Art Statum, who once, before a dodgeball game, warned that in the last class one boy had his collar bone dislocated during this activity. Coach Statum was so frightening to me that when he allowed us to go bowling one day, I decided to go bowling every gym class. As the term was ending, he showed up at the bowling alley and said: "Lynn, what are you doing here?" I told him he said we could go bowling, which he corrected. That was "for one class." Quickly figuring out what might save me, I showed him my bowling sheet and announced proudly, "Sorry, but look at how good I'm getting at this sport." He laughed.

Joanne and I spoke on the telephone to the couple that did the hiring for the summer nature job, Alfred and Naomi Shapiro, and discovered that they had first worked at Bear Mountain for their own honeymoon decades earlier. I reminded them again that we would be married just days before the start of the camp season. What a way to start married life, working from sunup to sundown side by side caring for animals and children. I did not blurt out that I couldn't tell a rattlesnake from a snapping turtle and said I felt that this job was going to work out, which it did.

We didn't see the Shapiros again for several weeks, but we moved to Bear Mountain State Park and the Lake Tiorati Nature Museum one Saturday in June 1970. The next day Mr. Shapiro showed up to see how we were doing in our log cabin with no inside toilet and camp-style twin metal beds at different heights—and he brought gifts.

The nature museum was to serve the two large camps in the vicinity of the place and show the largely inner-city young people what it was like to live in the woods for a few weeks. We were supposed to find live animals to populate the museum. The Shapiro visit got us started.

"Who wants this baby skunk?" Mr. Shapiro asked.

Joanne accepted the offer, while I was thinking, "What could be worse than a skunk?"

He also brought a large garbage can and said, "Here are some black snakes—which one do you want?"

The whole can was filled with writhing serpents. I knew these snakes were not poisonous and were less likely than most species to bite people even if annoyed. Nevertheless, I had never picked up a snake—so, with utterly false bravado, I told him to "give me the biggest one you have." Figuring, "In for a dime, in for a dollar," I draped the reptile around my neck and prayed dual wishes: that the creature could not sense fear and that it had eaten enough to feel lethargic. After that terrifying moment, I came to greatly admire snakes and to treasure my ability to handle them.

Over the next few days, we met the couples who were running the other four museums in the park, as well as the most "gung ho" camp counselor at the bigger of the two summer camps in our jurisdiction. The other people running museums seemed to have vastly greater knowledge of the natural order than I did, but the one couple that seemed to nail everything were Barry and Sally Oblas, he a biology teacher and she on her way to veterinary school. He wore a black leather jacket and made me uncomfortable.

My discomfort faded quickly when he asked if I wanted to go collect some animals to stock our museums. As we went exploring one afternoon, it seemed clear that he had no idea what he was doing. After about an hour, he told me that Shapiro had said that I was an expert on children and the environment. I told him I didn't know anything about nature, including how to catch frogs, raccoons, salamanders, or anything else. It became clear to both of us that Shapiro was setting us up to compete with each other. Not buying this competition, we decided to collaborate and help each other out.

The other Barry became a clinical psychologist and he and Sally eventually divorced, but we kept in touch with both of them for decades. I performed his second wedding, and Joanne visited Sally in a Michigan nursing home as she slipped into dementia.

It is one thing to fail to catch a frog, another to fail what the camp counselor wanted me to do: take his campers on a search for edible plants. This was serious because the wrong mushroom could poison someone. I spent almost a week reviewing books about plants and felt that I knew enough to get away with the hike. We saw birch trees whose twigs, steeped in hot water, made a tea tasting like birch beer, skunk cabbage, edible only if boiled multiple times, and wild mint.

We enjoyed interacting with almost all of the campers. They had two principal questions. One was snake specific: if its tongue touches me, will I die? The second, more generic, if it bites me, will it hurt? These young people came from some of the poorest neighborhoods in New York. Their only connection to wild animals was seeing pigeons and rats, so their questions weren't foolish at all.

This was our first summer as a married couple. We learned a few lessons. First, enjoy the work you are doing. My previous summer jobs were quite useless and unappealing. Second, enjoy the people you are working with. We had glorious, lengthy buffets together at a Viking-themed restaurant and late-night snacks at the Red Apple Rest on NY Route 9. Finally, even if you aren't initially qualified for a job, if you have a passion for that job and a determination to learn beyond the minimum, you will do just fine.

Joanne and I returned for a second summer there, as did Barry and Sally. That summer was one in which the bureaucracy of the park became the enemy. The apogee of our anger with them involved a young deer that briefly lived and then died on the screened porch of our rustic cabin. Counselors from one of the nearby camps had pulled this deer from a muddy section of the lake alongside a cliff, where it had been stuck and could not extricate itself. They pulled it out brought it to the "nature people" to handle. The animal seemed hurt, but the only thing we could do was keep it on our porch and try to feed it grain mixed with crushed antibiotic capsules. As it got sicker and sicker, we asked the park management to loan us a truck to transport it to a veterinarian about twenty miles away. They refused and the deer died. Campers came to visit the deer for the five days it lived on that porch—and then they watched us haul away its carcass. Lesson learned by children: Animals don't get help when they need it, so they aren't really that important. This was not a great environmental message.

Similar problems arose with the care of other animals, but none as dramatic as that deer's death. Barry Oblas and I tried to set up a meeting with the head of the park, but he was always "too busy" to see us. Finally, one afternoon we drove to his office, went into the foyer, and marched into his "inner sanctum," notwithstanding his assistant's pleading that this was a bad idea. He was surprised to see us, tried to calm us down, but ultimately never acknowledged that his office had done anything wrong. He told us to leave.

The story did not end here. Under the conditions of our employment contract, we had to write an article for publication by the State of New York about our experiences. There was no requirement that it be approved by the authorities. So, we wrote stinging rebukes of the park management. Joanne and I closed ours with a quotation from Malcolm X: "You are either part of the solution or you are part of the problem."

Our schedule did not permit us to return for a third summer, but I am quite confident we wouldn't have been rehired. Funding for this program ended in 1995, but Governor Andrew Cuomo reinstated a significant amount of state funding for parks and museums in 2021.

During that second summer I learned another lesson I've maintained for the rest of my life: never stop complaining about things you see that are wrong and enlist the press in your cause, even if you write articles yourself.

From the Woods to Boston

We arrived in Boston a few days before we were supposed to start classes at Boston University—Joanne at the medical school (BUSM) and me at the theology school (BUST). Why these acronyms appear to refer to breasts, I never figured out. Our first night was not propitious. We arrived in the dark and couldn't find a place to park our old car near the housing for married graduate students.

Our studio apartment had a reasonably large room with a Murphy bed that folded into the wall and gave the room a reasonably large appearance. When open, however, that bed took up the entire room. Joanne earned the ire of Boston University landlords by discovering that this building had layers of lead paint, which, as it peeled off, was particularly dangerous to children who might ingest the chips.

For fun we watched our 14-inch black and white television for which we paid $80. We got slices of pizza from a place called Yellow Submarine (complete with a Beatles mural) at the end of the block. And, of course, we had each other.

Aside from the conventional courses in Bible and theology, I needed to find several internships to gain some "practical experience." One worked out better than the others.

I had a weekly Monday session as a hospital chaplain at the prestigious Massachusetts General Hospital. On the first day I had a sit down with one of the experienced chaplains who asked what kind of patients I would like to see. My response was that I'd prefer to visit people who were likely to be hospitalized for a lengthy period, not folks who were in for a short time from a gunshot wound or a traffic accident. I was appropriately placed in a ward with chronic pain sufferers. The head chaplain warned me that one of the patients I'd be seeing was "becoming used to hospitalization" and would resist all efforts to go home. He had decided that she had become so acclimated to hospital life that she had developed a psychological barrier to returning home.

I visited her for several weeks. Her reluctance to go home seemed just what my supervisor had told me to expect. On the fourth week, I decided to confront this issue directly. I asked her what was keeping her in the hospital. She was blunt, "I live on the third floor of my apartment building. Who would possibly help carry my suitcase up that many stairs?" I told her I could help with that.

I started calling taxi companies the next day. I figured I might convince one to pick her up and that I'd go with her to carry the suitcase. I called from Cardinal Cushing Central High School where I had a simultaneous practicum, and the taxi dispatcher said, "There is no problem with this, and our driver will take up the suitcase, so you don't have to, Father." My counselee was ecstatic when I gave her the good news. She went home a few days later.

I learned two lessons from this. First, look for simple answers when complex answers turn out to be false. Second, I'd be better off finding practical help for people than merely assisting in their spiritual journeys. This inched me closer to a decision to find a night law school to attend.

The chaplaincy at Mass General was a mess at the time. One of my student chaplain colleagues said she had needed to leave a patient visit that morning because the patient was having blood drawn. Rather than explore this, a senior chaplain told her not to worry because he, too, couldn't stand the sight of blood. This seemed weird to me—why wouldn't a chaplain figure out how to deal with this aversion instead of telling others with the same issue that it was just fine to leave the room?

The professional chaplains infuriated almost all the interns that year. One student was badly injured when she was hit by a car close to graduation. She must have told her parents about the annoying chief chaplains. When one of them came to visit her in the hospital, her father told him he was not welcome to see her now or ever.

Before my stint at Massachusetts General Hospital, I had been a chaplaincy student at an alcohol rehabilitation center. I had plenty of long conversations with residents there and learned a key lesson: My limited life experience did not include addiction of any kind, leaving me little to offer. It dawned on me that seminaries might do a better job preparing students for personal encounters with people in need of help, people generally much older than the seminary students. It struck me that their failure was akin to instructing a second-year medical student to perform an appendectomy unsupervised.

The most important of my fieldwork projects was teaching at Cardinal Cushing Central High School for Girls (CCCH) in rock-solid Irish Catholic South Boston, "Southie" to its residents. This was one of the two Catholic schools that the archdiocese of Boston had wanted to make sure did not become havens for "white flight" when the public schools became racially integrated, something that seemed likely within a few years. Toward that end, CCCH began an aggressive scholarship program for African American and Hispanic students and went out of its way to hire non-Catholic teachers, both full-time and part-time, recruiting most of those part-time positions at a number of Boston-area theology schools.

During my interview with the head of the Religious Studies Department, I expressed an interest in teaching a bioethics course covering abortion, euthanasia, genetic engineering, and other hot button issues of the early Seventies. It turned out to be a quite popular course. I seemed to have a knack for simplifying complex moral issues for a high school audience. The students liked it and me and told other teachers and administrators that I was a "wonderful teacher."

Joanne and I attended a few parties arranged by members of the faculty, including one where I was told we were the only student teachers who had been invited. I enjoyed interacting with my fellow teachers in this way and learning more about them. How else would I have learned that Larry O'Toole of the biology department had an alligator living in his closet, to be bundled up in a towel and brought to school each spring? He also owned a boa constrictor who was fed by being taken to the Boston Common and sprinkled with popcorn—thus attracting pigeons who became his free lunch. These developments led the principal to offer me a paid position for the next two years, my teaching schedule to accommodate the classes I was taking.

We found an apartment in South Boston for the next few years. It was a comfortable one-bedroom apartment, except in the heat of the summer, since it had no air conditioning. On the day we moved in (with our $80 television), we watched the evening news. The news reported what was described as a "gangland style shooting" in a bar in Southie the previous night. As the television camera showed the façade of the bar, we thought it looked somewhat familiar, and I realized it was one of the two bars right next to our apartment building.

In that second year of teaching, I co-taught a course called Marriage and the Family with a recently divorced woman, ordinarily not permitted in most Catholic schools. We also had a question box where students could anonymously drop in inquiries they'd like us to answer. Some of them documented a profound misunderstanding of sexuality, but we treated each question with respect. One white student asked, "If I slept with a black man, could I have a mix-race baby even five years later?"

During my second year of teaching, I got a message in my faculty mailbox from the principal that she wanted to see me. When I got to her office, she got directly to the point, "Have you been having people from Planned Parenthood speak to your classes?" Indeed, I had, and they would usually bring samples of contraceptives with them. I surmised my honest answer would lead to my firing, but it did not. She said, "Well, I think it is important that our girls hear that stuff somewhere." The students' boyfriends I met while chaperoning several dances could also have used access to "that stuff." Planned Parenthood kept coming.

Young women (and some men) can push the envelope with male teachers by flirting with them. Male teachers must avoid even the appearance of being interested. As a kind of vaccination, I did an in-school version of the then-popular television show *The Newlywed Game* in which each member of a relatively newly married couple was asked a question and then compared that answer to the one given by the spouse. Joanne and I played the game and answered most of the student questions (a few were too personal or salacious) in a way that demonstrated that we were pretty familiar with each other and that I was not going to be interested in any flirtatious approaches.

Between my second and third year in Boston, we spent a summer in North Barnstead, NH, where Joanne had found work with a local physicians group, and I served a local summer-only church. We greatly enjoyed this creative, relaxed summer, our jobs, and our supportive community.

For the third year, I created a popular class called The Darker Side. Here is its description in the course booklet for the 1972-1973 year: "Would you like to try ESP experiments? Attempt to speak to the dead? Listen to a Black Mass? Participate in an exorcism to banish demons? The point of this course is to explain how psychic phenomena and the occult relate to the religious experience. We'll try to talk about things as diverse as the theory that God was really a visitor from outer space, experiments that claim to measure the weight of the soul as it leaves the body at death and the relationship between fate and the practice of astrology." It is still surprising to me that no parent objected to their daughter taking this class that contained little Christian theology.

I would occasionally have guest speakers, including George, a well-known South Boston psychic, who heard about the course and called me to see if he could speak to the class. Since I wanted to vet him, I invited him over for coffee one afternoon. We had a pet rabbit named Rapunzel ("Let down your long hare"). She spent most of her time in our bathroom but would come out when she heard the front door open to greet visitors. She only got halfway to George when she stopped abruptly, fell over, scrambled up, then turned and ran back to the bathroom. I said to George, "I don't know what psychic powers you have, but I have never seen her react to anyone this way."

George was a big hit in the class. Why didn't any parent object? The same course included a booklet with vivid descriptions of other classes including "Revolution and the Third World" and "Is God Dead?" Not your usual Catholic school offerings.

During the time I was teaching this course, William Friedkin's *The Exorcist* opened nationwide. The film was rated R and many of my students were not yet seventeen. I told all of them that I would be willing to serve as a guardian to get them into the showing if they provided a signed permission slip from one of their parents. I got over 100 of those slips and was, frankly, amazed that so many parents had nearly identical handwriting.

Come the day of the screening, Boston schools were all closed due to a snowstorm. I nevertheless considered it my duty to be at the theater just in case a few of my students showed up. When I got there, I found most of my students, many of whom brought their boyfriends. The screaming in the auditorium did not stop from the opening credits to the closing ones. It took me until the re-released, slightly longer version came out in 1979 to fully enjoy the film. I told this story to Eileen Dietz, the actress who substituted for Linda Blair in the scenes that Linda was too young to perform, like the masturbation with a crucifix scene. She was amused.

I spent three years teaching there. At the request of the seniors, I agreed to speak at their graduation in 1974. My speech was mainly about race. The local newspaper simply reported: "Barry Lynn spoke."

I remember one student vividly because of the circumstances under which she was trying to finish high school: She had been thrown out of her parents' house and had to find friends' floors on which to sleep. She spoke with me after class one day and said she was considering dropping out of school because she was not motivated enough to get out of bed. I told her that I was sorry to hear that and offered to call her each morning and check that she was planning to come to school. She said she'd try that, and for two weeks it seemed to work fine. Then in the third week she told me, "Thanks but I just can't do this anymore; I hope I can get my G.E.D. someday." I hope she did. In reflecting on this I doubt that this "call you in the morning" arrangement would be considered appropriate today; back then, I merely hoped that it would benefit one struggling young person.

Then, it was on to Washington DC to start that internship on amnesty.

Chapter 4

WORKING FOR THE UCC ON AMNESTY

Entering The Movement

My colleagues at Cardinal Cushing Central were delighted by my good employment luck. At a going away party a few weeks later, I joked that I was going to Washington to "build an empire." Several teachers came up to me afterward and said there was no doubt in their minds that such construction would occur. For me, it was just a joking reference.

In fact, I was petrified about beginning work. I had trouble even remembering the name of the church "instrumentality" I was working for. It was called the Center for Social Action. I knew nothing about Washington, about lobbying, or about church politics. I did know that, since the Vietnam War was morally wrong by any human standard, it was essential that there be a recognition of that from the United States government. I had even preached a sermon on the topic, one which sought to have the congregation, regardless of any member's view of the war, recognize that "forgiveness" was the "Christian" thing to do. I didn't think war resisters needed any forgiveness, but I was afraid saying it that way would take rural New Hampshire churchgoers too far out on a limb.

Almost immediately after my arrival in Washington, Fred Hofrichter, a church lobbyist, told me the whole "forgiveness" thing was not what the folks I'd be working with had in mind. An amnesty was a blotting out of the record, or, for many in this movement, a vindication of the moral and political truth that the war was a monstrous error, if not

53

a calculated crime against humanity. I felt better working with such an understanding. In fact, I was also convinced from the start that an amnesty would, like the Veterans of Foreign Wars claimed, make a draft in the future nearly impossible, because any draft-dodging miscreant would know that sooner or later the government would ignore what he had done.

My first day on the job consisted of crossing the lawn at the Capitol and finding copies of every bill dealing with Vietnam repatriation at the House Document Room, then visiting two Senate offices, and finally going to my first Washington cocktail party. For my first foray into lobbying, I stopped at the office of Michigan Senator Phil Hart. Bolstered mightily by his wife Jane, Hart had been one of the most articulate and passionate opponents of the war. He was working to prepare legislation that would resolve the dilemma of thousands of Vietnam Era draft and military resisters.

His legislative assistant, Don Tucker, was trying to craft legislation reflecting the call from pro-amnesty groups for a "universal, unconditional amnesty." This included upgrading all Vietnam-era "other than honorable" discharges, mostly given after perfunctory administrative hearings without counsel or due process. These "undesirable discharges" carried a stigma nearly as devastating as the "bad conduct" and "dishonorable" discharges given to those convicted at courts-martial. Don recognized the reality that few Senators were even willing to consider this issue, no matter how vigorous their vocal opposition to the conflict had been. There was, after all, still a war going on in Vietnam, albeit with limited American troop involvement. The visit to Hart's office was awe-inspiring because it appeared that Senator Hart was eager to get something moving, quickly.

I was so energized that, at Tucker's suggestion, I immediately popped in down the hall to the office of Democratic Senator James Abourezk of South Dakota. Since I had no appointment (and was wearing a cheap suit, to boot), I was surprised that the receptionist said the legislative director for the Senator would be happy to see me.

He was Tom Daschle, an earnest young man who promised that Abourezk would take Phil Hart's lead on this and do the right thing. (Daschle later became a Senator from South Dakota himself and was elected Majority Leader of the Senate). This was pretty heady: I had only been in Washington for a day, was sleeping on a mattress on the floor of our Arlington, Virginia, apartment, and felt that I had personally convinced 2% of the United States Senate to support near-total amnesty. I later realized that Daschle probably saw me only because so few people live in South Dakota that the office didn't have many visiting constituents.

Little wonder that I figured I deserved a trip to my first Washington cocktail party, an affair at the small African American history museum, honoring Congressman Robert Drinan (D/MA). This Jesuit priest/legislator had also been one of the harshest critics of the war and was the first to introduce articles of impeachment against Richard Nixon, not for the Watergate scandal that brought down his presidency, but for the illegal bombing of Cambodia. I had watched him at hearings the previous summer using the argumentative finesse of a Jesuit legal scholar to excoriate Administration officials still defending Nixon and/or the conflict in Southeast Asia. I was nervous about meeting him, but eventually I introduced myself and announced that the United Church of Christ had hired me to work full-time to lobby for amnesty. He offered a response both curt and polite: "Well, it's about time."

Many years later, at a gathering of religious leaders in Washington, following a speech by Drinan, I asked him what he thought of recent disclosures that the Federal Bureau of Investigation was opening files on "liberal" religious activists, he wryly commented, "Maybe with people like you around, Barry, they should." The crowd got the joke and roared approval. Drinan later left Congress after a Papal decree that priests could not serve in the legislature of any country. He went on to teach at Georgetown University Law Center and serve as the chairman of Common Cause.

Senator Hart convened a special briefing on amnesty at which I testified, along with many other advocates and a few opponents. He articulated his support for amnesty at a Senate Judiciary Committee hearing as well. That hearing was one of the few that Joanne was able to attend. When we went up to see him after the testimony and questioning was completed, she asked, "How do you take on so many controversies at the same time?" He simply responded, "Sometimes you just have to do what is right." I have never forgotten those words.

At the time of that hearing, Senator Hart was undergoing treatment for cancer, and within a few months he died, on December 26, 1976. His wife Jane got a phone call from President Gerald Ford who asked if there was anything he could do for her. She calmly said, "Phil would have wanted you to grant amnesty for Vietnam War resisters." Ford said he would consider it.

This interchange was so powerful that it was the top of the news for hours on the Sunday night it was disclosed. I was in Bethlehem visiting my parents but left a little early when I got a call from Gold Star Mother Louise Ransom, who said Ms. Hart had wanted a few of us to join her at a press conference the next day. I had never seen so many television cameras at a press conference. Ms. Hart was eloquent and the rest of us made brief remarks. To my knowledge, there was no coverage of the event on any of the nightly news shows. Cable news was in its infancy and, of course, the internet did not exist. President Ford called Ms. Hart a few days later and told her he could not honor her request but promised to consider other options.

The people I met and worked with were extraordinary women and men. There was Louise Ransom, whose husband was a top lawyer for IBM and whose son was killed in Vietnam in 1968. Louise and other Gold Star Mothers like Patricia Simon in Massachusetts and Peg Mullin in Iowa were ceaseless activists for amnesty despite the deaths of their sons.

President Ford's Earned Re-Entry Program

Ford set up something called the "Earned Re-Entry Program," a clemency program that turned out to be a total failure. He announced its creation at a convention of the Veterans of Foreign Wars in 1974, noting that persons who could participate in his program had "committed the supreme folly of shirking their duty at the expense of others." In order to gain any benefit, Ford's proposal required the "shirker" to "earn" his way back to society by engagement in "alternate service," the length to be determined by a Presidential Clemency Board. The Board was headed by former moderate Republican Senator from New York, Charles Goodell, and included a raft of other members. A few of them, like Notre Dame President Father Theodore

Hesburgh and Democratic African American political insider Vernon Jordan, had credibility on some progressive issues. In a cover story for the progressive magazine *Christianity and Crisis*, I called Ford's Earned Re-entry Program "Not Exactly an Olive Branch."

Presumably as a favor to Hesburgh, Ford gave a major speech on foreign policy at Notre Dame that set out a fairly belligerent analysis of the United States' role in the world. Hesburgh himself maintained that he was helping unfortunate persons, while people in what he called the "full amnesty movement" leaders just "sit in the corner and pout." I went to a lecture given by Vernon Jordan in Washington at about that time. Mingling with the audience after the event, I went up to Jordan, who had endorsed a genuine amnesty months earlier, and suggested he resign from the Board, noting that it was the lawyers in Nazi Germany who did not sign up for service on the sterilization courts that history remembered as heroes of that period. He didn't take it well. This may have been an inappropriate parallel, but the German lawyers who did serve used the argument that "at least we could do some good for some people," the same argument that Jordan tended to make. As to the "pouting" amnesty leaders that Hesburgh mentioned, I saw only a renewed commitment to increased organizing and advocacy tied to the obvious failure of Ford's program.

Henry Schwarzschild, then working at the American Civil Liberties Union in New York City, was the head of its Project on Amnesty. I had seen him on several television debates and was so impressed that I was a bit reticent to meet him for the first time. I wore a green checkered polyester suit, the only arguably appropriate attire for a brief period in the Seventies. He asked why I was going to law school. After I explained my sense that it would help me help others who needed more legal help than spiritual solace, he said, "Okay, but never forget that any issue worth thinking about for more than a minute is not ultimately a legal issue." I never forgot that because laws contain moral values, one's own moral center must determine whether those values are good ones.

Duane Shank of the National Interreligious Service Board for Conscientious Objectors taught me about how to message these issues and put me in touch with many of the veterans and persons in exile who worked every day for the justice that resisters deserved. Indeed, Duane invited me to his office the day Ford announced his program so I could call a war resister in Canada named Gerry Condon, who explained to a reporter for the local Fox affiliate over the phone why he wasn't taking Ford's offer. Gerry had been trained as a Green Beret but left the Army when he understood that he would soon be asked to take aggressive actions against innocent civilians.

Irma Zigas was one of the founders of Women Strike for Peace, along with Cora Weiss and Bella Abzug who would later become a member of Congress. Irma became the director of the umbrella group, the National Council for Universal Unconditional Amnesty. When the Ford program failed, she said, "Before the Congress will move those of us who spent so much time on counseling people about the punitive nature of the Ford clemency program, we will need to do even more local educational and organizing work to achieve a universal amnesty with no strings attached."

And that was what we did, recognizing that the 1976 presidential campaign might be our last chance to get any real resolution of the issue.

A number of war resisters in Canada were associated with the magazine *Amex/Canada* (as in "American exiles in Canada"). It was a chronicle of anti-war activity and laid out the facts about what a genuine amnesty would mean. Steve Grossman, its original editor, became the largely unwilling poster child for amnesty. He never seemed comfortable with things like appearing on the cover of *The New York Times Magazine*, or the prospect that he would be the subject of a made-for-television movie with Richard Thomas, John Boy from the successful series *The Waltons*, playing him. Grossman had been indicted for refusal to be drafted but, after a successful legal battle, he returned to the United States and went on a series of speaking tours to generate support for anti-militarism.

Amex/Canada also had key writers and editors Dee Knight and Gerry Condon, both of whom spent the rest of their lives in activities against American imperialism and racial injustice. Dee recently published a memoir called *My Whirlwind Lives: A Political Memoir & Manifesto–Navigating Decades of Storms*. Jerry became president of the widely respected organization, Veterans for Peace.

What was so bad about Ford's Earned Re-Entry Program? Let me count the ways. As memoranda leaks of Defense and Justice Department documents clearly indicated, these agencies were operating fundamentally punitive programs, often harsher than alternatives in the court system that existed before the clemency program was even announced.

The Justice Department handled all Vietnam era draft law violators who had not been convicted. An individual was told to contact the U.S. Attorney in the district in which he committed, or believed he might have committed, the "offense" of resisting the draft. He was asked to accept up to two years of alternate service so that he would not be prosecuted. However, the government did not have to prove that a person was actually guilty of any Selective Service violation.

For example, the first alleged draft violator to turn himself in was John Barry of San Francisco, who discovered when he presented himself to the U.S. Attorney there that, not only was he unindicted, he was not even under investigation. Of course, to prevent an investigation and prompt indictment from occurring, he had to pledge to complete alternate service.

The Justice Department had a notoriously hard time successfully prosecuting alleged draft evaders. Thousands of indictments were dropped during the earlier decade because of a lack of evidence or procedural errors in the Selective Service process. Many of those currently in exile or living underground in the United States had already had their cases dismissed but were never informed by the Justice Department. By 1973, even the relatively few convicted resisters were treated somewhat leniently. Only 37% were given any prison time, and their terms averaged only 17.5 months, with parole available for many to shorten those sentences. Therefore, requiring the punishment in the clemency plan without a U.S. Attorney having to prove that an offense had been committed was tantamount to short-circuiting the entire judicial system.

Several days after the program was announced, the Justice Department virtually admitted that the whole program was of questionable constitutionality. But, U.S. Attorneys insisted that persons accepting the clemency program would need to sign a waiver of many of their constitutional rights, including the right to due process, speedy trial, consideration of any statute of limitations, and protection against double jeopardy.

The Defense Department was to handle all military absentees of the Vietnam era who had no additional charges pending. DoD was to process them through Fort Benjamin Harrison in Indianapolis. The processing included their reaffirmation of allegiance "to the Government and the Constitution," a pledge to fulfill up to twenty-four months of alternate service, and the receipt upon completion of an "undesirable discharge." For a time, the Defense Department claimed that they never intended to require men to complete their alternate service unless they wanted to be able to exchange their "undesirable" discharge for a newly minted "clemency discharge."

That position changed, and affected persons were told that, if the alternate service was not completed, there was the possibility they would be prosecuted under Article 83 of the Uniform Code of Military Justice, which prohibits fraudulently obtaining a discharge. Of course, during the period before the policy change, many persons returned to accept their "undesirable" discharge precisely because they believed Secretary of Defense James R. Schlesinger's initial claims that no service would actually be required.

This change of policy probably came about when it became clear that the "clemency discharge" was no better—and might be even worse—than an "undesirable" one. The clemency discharge granted no Veterans Administration benefits, marked a person for life as a "deserter," albeit a repentant one, and could not be appealed to obtain a possible upgrade. An "undesirable" discharge at least permitted some benefits on a discretionary basis by governmental agencies, left some doubt as to why it was issued (employers occasionally recognized that serious personality clashes alone between the recipient and his commanding officer can lead to an undesirable discharge), and could be appealed and upgraded by a Discharge Review Board at the Pentagon after a full hearing where counsel was permitted.

As with civilian resisters, Army absentees, who made up the bulk of the eligible military, also had always had alternatives. They had been able to obtain what were known as "Chapter 10" discharges after less than a month of confinement (or none at all). Chapter 10s are "undesirable" discharges given in lieu of a court martial "for the good of the service." These could be appealed. Many absentees clearly realized that the Ford approach gave them a form of discharge at least as bad as a court martial, despite their serving a full two years of punitive action. They would have received a few *weeks* of military control under court martial.

Ironically, military absentees still had the option of trying to obtain a Chapter 10 discharge, and legal aid was available to fight one's absenteeism charge through a court martial, perhaps even obtaining a discharge under honorable conditions. One JAG officer, i.e., a military lawyer at Benjamin Harrison, conceded to *The New York Times* that as many as half of returnees could travel this route successfully and end up with an honorable discharge, but most were too confused or tired to bother.

Absentees who even inquired about their status were subject to problems. Any information given over the phone or by mail to the clemency processing agency at Benjamin Harrison Center could and would be used against the absentee if he failed to report by January 31, 1975.

Making Public the List of "Offenders"

In 1974, the Justice Department released a list of 6,200 men still wanted for draft offenses. For years, Justice had denied the existence of such a list; under pressure from Senator Edward Kennedy (D/MA), they begrudgingly released one. When the Presidential Clemency Board began, I called about a man I was counseling to see if he was eligible. The person answering the phone said she'd "know in a minute" by "checking our list." When I learned his status, I suggested that that list be turned over to counseling groups since indictments are public records. A Freedom of Information Act request led fairly quickly to a computerized printout of names.

After a few days of deciphering codes on the list, we realized that the list was not only of indicted persons but also of persons still under investigation by the FBI. Senator Kennedy took a great interest in this list and got the Justice Department to agree that it would stop investigating Selective Service violations and produce a definitive list of those actually indicted. Thousands of people thought they had been indicted because their names were on the list when actually they had not been. The release of the "final list" that was distributed to a few counseling groups, the ACLU, and me, proved to be of enormous interest to those who could now know their status.

United States Senate

COMMITTEE ON THE JUDICIARY
SUBCOMMITTEE ON
ADMINISTRATIVE PRACTICE AND PROCEDURE
(PURSUANT TO SEC. 1, S. RES. 16, 110 CONGRESS)
WASHINGTON, D.C. 20510

January 24, 1975

Center for Social Action
The United Churches of Christ
110 Maryland Avenue, NE
Washington, D.C. 20002

Gentlemen:

The attached list contains the names of individuals who are presently charged by indictment, information or complaint, and those who are under investigation for draft offenses (other than non- or late registration) during the Vietnam era. This list is being provided to your organization, pursuant to your letter to me of January 21, 1975, for the sole purpose of conveying information from the list only to individuals, their families, or representatives. It is understood that you will not generally publicize the names on this list.

I appreciate your cooperation in this effort.

Sincerely,

Edward M. Kennedy
Chairman

Enclosure

Senator Edward Kennedy got the Justice Department to release the names of all persons liable for federal prosecution for violations of the Military Selective Service Act and distributed it to a few organizations including the United Church of Christ. Thousands of men who thought they were in legal jeopardy could determine definitively if they were in legal peril, and many were not.

The Clemency Board was to deal exclusively with persons already convicted of draft resistance or already discharged with an "Undesirable," "Bad Conduct," or "Dishonorable" discharge due to absenteeism. The convicted draft felon who applied to the Board may have been asked to do two additional years of "service," but even this did not result in the expungement of his felony criminal record. Ray Mitchell, an attorney with the Clemency Board, said that, although this clemency would "probably" restore federal civil rights, you would still need to state on employment applications that you are a felon, even if you are a felon for resisting the draft. That effectively closed whole occupations to people who received this clemency. This included such blue-collar jobs as barbering or taxi-driving, occupations that excluded felons from obtaining licenses.

The power of the Clemency Board for redress of bad discharges was similarly constrained. Only absenteeism-related discharges could be considered. Anti-war or anti-racism GIs who peacefully protested America's Indochina policies in demonstrations or underground newspapers who had been court-martialed would have no redress, unless they had combined their protest with desertion.

Few people who participated in the Ford program got much of anything. Many of the first group of "deserters" who did seek redress there spoke to *The Christian Science Monitor* and were surprised to learn of the options I described above.

In early January 1975, I appeared at a press conference with former Attorney General Ramsey Clark to respond to the release of the official Report of the Clemency Board. I called the document "a whitewash designed to make a vindictive program appear magnanimous." At this event, I pointed out that the Selective Service System had a miserable record of locating jobs for participants, with fewer than 28% of those eligible for a work assignment ever starting their jobs. The jobs available to those in the clemency program had to be "non-competitive" and "in the public interest." Although not a null set, this was an extremely tiny number of jobs.

I also demonstrated that the Clemency Board was inefficiently managed. The President was to give final approval to applicants' terms of service, but at this point, thousands of cases were still awaiting Ford's actions. Moreover, the cases heard by the Board were often prepared by staff members with no expertise in military or draft law. Therefore, they were incapable of fully evaluating an individual's case. Panels of Board members sometimes considered as many as 125 cases in a day, with no personal appearances by applicants before the Panels. Indeed, it turned out that some cases were heard by two different panels and resulted in two different decisions!

At the time, Wisconsin Democratic Senator William Proxmire was obsessed with the removal of wasteful government spending. He issued Golden Fleece awards for particularly useless expenditures. I suggested he look at the record of the Board and perhaps give it a Golden Fleece of the Year shout out. I told him, "This was a $6-million-dollar boondoggle that gave its chairman national publicity, its top staffers access to a $225,000 grant from the Ford Foundation to study the program they ran, and its applicants one of the worst deals in town." Proxmire politely declined my suggestion.

Father Hesburgh was instrumental in getting the chief administrative architects of the Clemency Board process, Lawrence Baskir and William Strauss, the grant to study its own work. Hesburgh himself wrote the preface to the book they produced called *Chance and Circumstance*. He had the gall to claim that if enough Americans "read this book and ponder its implications, I am sure we may then legitimately put the Vietnam experience behind us, for we will have restored justice to what is now a very unjust residue of a very unpopular war."

I hated most of this book, and said so in a review in *Inquiry* magazine: It "lacks any philosophical or ideological coherence and is characterized by a veiled but smirking arrogance toward those people whose lives were shattered by Vietnam." A great deal of the book was an effort to trivialize the anti-war and draft resistance movement and to make extreme comments about the amnesty movement itself. Baskir and Strauss claimed that the "end of the Ford program saw the collapse of much of the vitality of the amnesty movement." This was flatly untrue as the Ford program was so useless that it only contributed to congressional efforts on amnesty and popular support for a better resolution and pressures on the next (presumably Democratic) President to act responsibly.

One of the few good things to come out of the book was a mounting awareness of how few men of the "Vietnam generation" actually served during that period. Although 26,800,000 men were eligible for service, only 10,935,000 enlisted or were drafted; of these, only 1,600,000 saw combat. A related conclusion in the book was that poorly educated, low-income whites and persons of color bore a disproportionate share of Vietnam-era service, injuries, and deaths. This had been pointed out by antiwar activists for years, but the book gave ballast to this reality.

References in the Report to how "nothing...should be used to infer improper activity by any government agency in the past" were particularly appalling. This completely ignored the blatant lawlessness of many in the Selective Service System and the abusive nature of much of "military justice," to say nothing of the criminal conduct of the wars in Indochina—the very factors that led to war resistance in the first place and the need for amnesty.

I also rejected the value of certain statistical conclusions that were based almost entirely on participants in the program, ignoring the vast number of people who boycotted the program. Also ignored was the real concern I and many others heard from participants who downplayed their anti-war motivations out of fear that certain Board members might treat them more harshly because of their anti-military beliefs.

Skirmishes and Strategies

Notwithstanding the release of the "definitive" list of draft resisters in legal jeopardy by Senator Kennedy, by February 1975 federal authorities at the Immigration and Naturalization Service (INS) indicated that a section of the Immigration and Nationality Act could be interpreted to prevent some war resisters from ever returning to the United States, even for a visit.

Section 212(a)(22) of the Act bars entry to anyone who became a citizen of another country and left or remained abroad to "avoid or evade training or service in the armed forces." The INS was claiming that the thousands of American men who became naturalized citizens of Canada, Sweden or other nations in recent years would be presumed to have left to avoid military service. This procedure simply ignored the thousands of cases in which alleged draft resisters had investigations terminated or indictments dismissed because those offenses could not be proven as a matter of law. INS decided that, notwithstanding decisions by prosecutors, it could lawfully assume that obtaining citizenship was an act to avoid serving in the military. As I told the National Council of the Churches of Christ's Special Ministries of the Vietnam Generation at that time, " If there was ever any doubt that the Clemency Program was not designed to heal or reconcile, now the government is saying: Even if federal prosecutors no longer consider you a draft dodger, we will have the immigration service declare you to be one anyway!" Essentially this was a pernicious way to bar persons from even visiting their former home. I cautioned, "The American people and the American Congress must now choose between a real 'amnesty' without strings or conditions, or 'revenge.' The National Council of Churches is squarely on the side of 'amnesty,' heeding the warning from the book of Leviticus: 'You shall not seek vengeance, nor bear any grudge against the sons of your own people.'"

Thus began a full-blown effort on the part of amnesty advocates to get Congress to act. I was on the board of the National Council for a Universal, Unconditional Amnesty (NCUUA), but some other members of that body were a bit uncomfortable with my support of some legislative initiatives and the arguments raised by those legislators. Nevertheless, the Board asked me to keep it appraised of all congressional initiatives.

By early 1975, thirty-one members of the House had become co-sponsors or voiced support of an amnesty bill led by Congresswoman Bella Abzug (D/NY). It would cover anti-war resisters whose alleged crimes occurred between January 1, 1961, when significant numbers of so-called "advisers" were working with the South Vietnamese military, and November 22, l974, when the last draftee was released from military service. The bill included an automatic general amnesty for Selective Service law resisters and any military personnel who were "deserters-at-large" or who had been discharged for virtually all offenses in the Uniform Code of Military Justice that would not be crimes in civilian life (including absentee offenses, disrespect for officers, insubordination, and others). The remedies in this bill included a full restoration of civil rights, protection against future prosecution, an uncoded Honorable Discharge for those in the military, and nullification of any other legal consequences, such as having to report being a felon to future employers.

Abzug's bill also dealt with civilian war resisters by creating an "amnesty commission" to evaluate claims for violation of "any Federal law...or state or local law" if the violation was motivated by opposition to American participation in Indochina and did not result in "significant property damage or substantial personal injury to others." Despite my opposition to having case-by-case reviews in most circumstances, as I wrote in a memo at the time, "We could have John Mitchell and H.R. Haldeman claiming that their Watergate-related offenses were motivated by opposition to the war in Vietnam. Intriguing as any flat grant of amnesty in the non-draft law world would be, amnesty is not a viable answer for totally emptying out America's jails."

The National Council for a Universal, Unconditional Amnesty would not endorse the Abzug bill. I was in the NCUUA offices in New York when its director, Irma Zigas, got a call from the Congresswoman who literally screamed so loudly that I could hear across the room about how angry she was that the coalition would not unequivocally endorse her legislation.

In the Senate, Senators Hart (D/MI), McGovern (D/SD), and Nelson (D/WI) had introduced legislation to grant an automatic elimination of adverse consequences for all categories of resisters covered by the Ford program. The bill was written to avoid being sent to the Senate Armed Services Committee, a boneyard for any progressive idea. Instead, it was sent to the Judiciary Committee, whose members included Hart and a host of progressive Democrats and Republican Charles "Mac" Mathias (R/MD), who were inclined to support the Hart bill. This bill (and the Abzug proposal) would have provided a means for Americans who had become citizens of another country to either become United States citizens again or obtain visitation rights that were barred by the INS law provision.

In March 1976, I spoke to a briefing for the WISC/IMPACT congressional briefing. This was an annual ecumenical gathering of progressive religious activists. I reiterated the magnitude of the need for an unconditional amnesty and the failure of the Ford clemency program. I noted that Senator Phil Hart had said, a few days earlier, that Congress was not failing to act because it was concerned that it lacked the constitutional authority to do so, it was failing to act because "we the Congress do not have the guts to act."

I also mentioned that a year earlier, during the admission to the United States of many thousands of Vietnamese refugees, General Ngo Dzu was admitted, who had long been identified as a principal heroin trafficker in Southeast Asia. I pointed out that it "does not make sense to continue to punish the 30,000 American G.I. addicts who were victims of his criminality with a less than honorable discharge which keeps them unemployed and quite likely deprives them of access to a V.A. hospital for treatment." In addition, major American corporations in the hotel and recreation business were negotiating with the Vietnamese government for ways to generate tourist visits to Vietnam. I noted, "It is absurdly immoral, while these business negotiations go on, to continue to keep Americans in exile so they cannot even visit their own homeland to grieve at their mother's funeral."

I had been on a television show hosted on PBS by Martin Agronsky the night before Senator Hart's congressional briefing, along with the national security director of the Veterans of Foreign Wars, Colonel Phelps Jones. I mentioned that it took Robert E. Lee 107 years to be amnestied and regain his citizenship for his participation as the lead military figure for the Confederacy in the Civil War. After we left the stage, Jones said that was about the length of time appropriate for a Vietnam amnesty as well.

Polling data suggested that anyone who would win the Democratic Party nomination for President in 1976 would have to support some kind of legal relief for war resisters and the entire "pro-amnesty" movement promoted that idea. Jimmy Carter indicated that he would act on this matter, although it was unclear exactly how.

President Jimmy Carter's Executive Order on Amnesty.

To push forward on this, we had a plan to make a major statement at the 1976 Democratic Convention in New York City. We would nominate as Vice President a draft resister named Fritz Efaw, who had been in exile in England but who had been elected as an alternate delegate to the Convention. After extensive organizing by Dee Knight and others at NCUUA, Efaw returned to the United States at Kennedy Airport, where he was met by a large contingent of press, many supporters, and a few federal marshals. A New York federal magistrate had ordered the marshals to let Efaw attend the Convention and make an appearance on *Good Morning America.* Many pro-amnesty volunteers got enough signatures to permit him to be nominated. Steve Grossman, who had some theatrical experience, readily convinced all of us that we needed him nominated by—and that nomination seconded by—people who would hold the attention of television viewers, since this whole process would unfold in prime time the day before the Carter acceptance speech. Those nominators were Ron Kovic, a decorated Marine who had lost both legs in Vietnam, David Addlestone, a military law expert and former prisoner of war, and Louise Ransom, whose son had been killed in Vietnam on Mothers Day, 1968.

Kovic was in a wheelchair. When some of us went to the Democratic Party officials to tell them our plans, they initially told us that a person in a wheelchair could not get up on the podium. This laughable claim was, we pointed out, belied by the fact that the Convention's opening night included a talk by George C. Wallace, the former Governor of Alabama, at that time still deeply racist. Wallace had been paralyzed by a bullet from a would-be assassin, and the Convention had managed to get him to the podium. They relented. Party officials made other efforts to stop this process, including changing the rules of delegate signatures required and claiming Efaw was too young to meet Constitutional requirements.

My assignment was to return to Washington and appear on the most important "news talk" television show at the time, *Panorama* with Maury Povich. Povich did lots of hard news at the time and was not the "let's do a polygraph about your adultery" guy he later became. I was supposed to tell his audience that there would be a big surprise that night at the Convention involving Fritz Efaw. Maury, whose show I had been on numerous times, said bluntly, "Barry, the Democratic Party is never going to let a 'surprise' happen." I told him with some trepidation, based on my already developing perception that Democrats could default to spinelessness, "I guarantee it will occur."

The nomination by Ron and Louise and Fritz' "acceptance speech" went off perfectly, and an iconic picture of Ron holding up his arms in an embrace with the words printed that he had uttered that night "Welcome Home, Fritz" became a fundraising and educational postcard for the amnesty movement for the months prior to the election.

In dramatic fashion, Vietnam Veteran Ron Kovic was nominated Vietnam draft resister Fritz Efaw for U.S. Vice President at the 1968 Democratic National Convention.
Source: Getty Images

The depiction of this event in *Born on the Fourth of July* was not completely accurate because it showed the convention in full-blown approval of what was happening. Although I was still in Washington and watched the fruits of their labor on television, some of the activists described booing and clearly intentional walkouts by some politicians. Sara Kovner, a highly respected New-York based fundraiser for Democrats and progressive causes who had initially backed Congressman Morris K. "Mo" Udall of Arizona for the Presidency, told me she ran after Udall as he walked away and screamed, "I am sorry I ever supported you."

Amnesty in the Carter Presidency

The outcome of the election was never clear cut. For those of us waiting in a Washington hotel ballroom, things were not going well until the delayed vote count in New York was announced, which gave Carter that rich electoral college delegation, giving him 41 of the 297 electoral votes that won him the presidency.

For the amnesty advocates, it was time for the hard work of making sure that Carter's "transition team" understood both the magnitude of what needed done, and that they needed to act quickly, lest conservatives in Congress try to block amnesty as soon as they began legislating. I had heard rumors of this and, sure enough, once a Carter pardon was imminent, Democratic Senator from Alabama James Allen spent the first three weeks of January—when Congress convenes but before the President is inaugurated on January 20—trying to pass a "Sense of the Senate" resolution that Carter not act.

After the election itself, a delegation of activists, including the President of the National Council of Churches, Presbyterian minister Bill Thompson, who had served on the United States tribunal examining Japanese war crimes; Henry Schwarzschild; Louise Ransom; Ron Kovic; David Addlestone, military law expert; former Prisoner of War Colonel Edison Miller; and I traveled to Atlanta to speak with Charles Kirbo, a partner in the prestigious law firm of King and Spaulding, who was coordinating Carter's political entry into Washington. Kirbo listened well and seemed to understand the legal and moral issues involved.

Kovic told Kirbo, "I need to believe in this country again." He told reporters, "We might have real changes in this country." We were guardedly optimistic. The new administration assigned Houston attorney David Berg to work on amnesty policy.

I worked a great deal with Berg, who seemed to be a genuinely empathetic and reasonable person. He wrote the pardon to cover all violators or potential violators of the draft laws, from the day of the fabricated Tonkin Gulf resolution in 1964, until the day the last United States forces left the country in 1973. This covered 9,700 men who had been convicted. It also effectively "amnestied" the roughly 4,000 men who were under indictment or investigation for Selective Service law violations and an estimated 100,000 who had never registered with Selective Service. It also remedied Nixon's change to immigration law that had barred persons who had acquired foreign citizenship "to avoid the draft" from entering the United States. Presidential pardon power does not extend to restoring citizenship, but the change permitted entry into the United States with the possibility of reapplying for U.S. citizenship. All this was done through an Executive Order on Inauguration Day, January 20, 1977.

On January 22, something went wrong. I got a call in the middle of that Saturday afternoon from a person who represented a man who had been pardoned and tried to return to attend his grandmother's funeral. Officials at the U.S.-Canada border would not allow him to cross, arguing that he was not only on the "watch list" for draft resistance (which was pardoned) but also on the list for an entirely separate crime—"flight to avoid prosecution," for which no pardon had been issued. Thousands of people were in that same category. We had wrongly assumed that such a directly tied collateral offense would also be pardoned, but that proved to be a false assumption. "What can you do?" he asked.

It was four o'clock on a Saturday afternoon and I had no home phone numbers for anyone in the Carter Administration. Although I assumed it was a fool's errand, I placed a call to the White House switchboard and asked to be put through to the office of Counsel to the President, Bob Lipshutz. The phone rang dozens of times and was picked up by a man with a strong Southern accent. He said "Bob Lipshutz."

I said: "We haven't met, but I strongly supported President Carter. I'm calling about a pardon-related problem that could prove very embarrassing to the President." He listened and said he'd "take care of it immediately." He prepared an order that pardoned any minor collateral offenses related to draft evasion. On CBS' *Face the Nation* program the next day, he was asked how the pardon was working and noted that there was "one small problem" that had already been resolved.

Most U.S. Attorneys were holdovers from the Nixon-Ford years, and a few dug in with their opposition, one actually arguing that a man could still be prosecuted for theft of government property for leaving an induction center with blank medical forms he had been asked to fill out. The one collateral offense that was not pardoned was for the one man who set his draft board on fire the day he refused induction.

All in all, the pardon for draft resisters was good for persons who wanted to clean up their record and possibly re-obtain federal benefits. It did not expunge criminal records and many principled opponents of the war felt it was unconscionable for them to apply to receive a pardon, insisting correctly that they had done nothing wrong and should have received an amnesty that would have removed any trace of negative consequences. Years later, I met the long-time acoustic music critic for the *Boston Globe*, Scott Alarick, who told me that he was among the hard-to-determine number of men who had refused to apply for this relief.

The other major deficiency in Carter's action was the timeframe for relief. Although it may have taken Congress until August 1964 to realize there was a war in Southeast Asia, a sizeable number of young Americans had a very good idea of what was happening much earlier. Between January 1961, when the first Green Beret/CIA "advisors" were acknowledged to have entered Vietnam, and the Tonkin Gulf incident, more than 600 persons were convicted of Selective Service violations. In one poignant letter I received, the writer said: "Right after I graduated from high school in 1964, I could tell from the higher draft calls that we were heading into war. I walked across the border, though, one month too early." Many of these early resisters were traditional religious objectors.

Just a few days after the pardon was announced, Lipshutz told CBS that to "heal another wound" from Vietnam, the Administration would quickly conduct a study of how to deal with military resisters and veterans with other-than-honorable discharges. Two factors complicated the study. First, the Carter Administration wanted to see what the reaction to the pardon was. In the week following the announcement, the Administration got only 4,800 letters on the subject, with roughly 3,000 of them opposing the action. One decorated veteran threw his medals over the White House fence, a state American Legion convention voted to throw President Carter out of the organization, several VFW members publicly burned their honorable discharges, and several members of Congress filed an unsuccessful lawsuit challenging the Presidential action as unconstitutional.

Second, Father Hesburgh met with Carter twice to advocate for a complicated review program developed by Baskir and Strauss, staff on the failed Ford Clemency Board, which involved issuing a new kind of general discharge that included no veterans' benefits. It was a dopey creature that was described by Duane Shank of the National Interreligious Service Board for Conscientious Objectors as of "truly insignificant benefit to most veterans, when there are 750,000 stigmatized veterans who need genuine relief in the form of an honorable discharge."

David Berg, the Administration lawyer who wrote the pardon legislation, was himself initially opposed to granting any relief to military "deserters," since opinion polls showed that relief for deserters was much less popular than draft resister pardons. I spent a lot of time with him at the White House along with Tom Alder, the publisher of the *Selective Service Law Reporter* and the *Military Law Reporter* (which, years later, I edited) and others. One morning leaving a White House meeting, Tom and I were stopped by ABC's Sam Donaldson to find out what we could tell him about the new "energy policy."

Berg changed his mind about "deserters" and also felt that it would be fair, and even good financially, to automatically upgrade all 160,000 administratively granted "undesirable discharges." Berg convinced top Carter advisor, Stuart Eizenstadt, that the military deserters and those discharged with punitive consequences should be granted relief. Berg told me once that when he spoke to Carter, the President was not very sympathetic and said, "If I had been called up to go to Vietnam I would have gone and stayed."

The program announced in March 1977 allowed 4,000 who deserted from non-combat zones during the 1963-1973 period to be "processed out" within three days. The program contained some remarkably liberal features like toll-free numbers to ascertain eligibility and letters that authorized entry into the United States at border crossings. The combat zone restriction was purely for public relations purposes because almost no one left a battle in the jungles—except in movies—but even leaving from rest and relaxation breaks in Japan or from hospitalization was often considered leaving from combat. Nevertheless, 95% of military absentees–the 4,000 or so "deserters at large" whose existence the Department of Defense admitted–were eligible and many chose to obtain relief. The discharge question became much more complicated, though, and was only partially resolved years later by the actions of Senators Ed Brooke (R/MA) and Jim Abourezk (D/SD).

The review of military discharges announced at the same time was largely window dressing that avoided coming to terms with the reality of military justice during most of the Vietnam Era. It gave only those with administrative discharges the right to ask that their cases be reviewed and barred the 35,000 persons given Bad Conduct or Dishonorable discharges by courts-martial from having their cases reviewed. Whether you were quickly mustered out or tried by court-martial often depended solely on who was your commanding officer. Tens of thousands of military members who had addiction disorders were given administrative discharges but, in the early years of the war, several thousand were court-martialed for drug use. Even those who were declared AWOL often got administrative discharges late in the war, while several thousand others were court-martialed for the same offense. Some commanders wanted to use the harsher treatment as an example to other service members. I met many people convicted of so-called crimes that had no civilian counterpart. Four Marines were convicted of "provoking gestures" because they flashed a peace sign.

Three soldiers at the Phu Cat Air Force Base witnessed Korean troops skinning a Vietnamese prisoner and threw down their guns in front of their commanding officer. He then insisted they go on patrol unarmed, which they did for three nights before being court martialed and given bad conduct discharges for "insubordinate conduct toward a non-commissioned officer." Roger Priest was awarded a bad conduct discharge for "bringing discredit upon the armed forces" for publishing anti-war newspapers. Dr. Howard Levy violated Article 133 of the Uniform Code of Military Justice, "conduct unbecoming an officer and a gentleman," when he refused to train Green Beret medics. This is dissent, not a crime—but he was not eligible for relief under the Carter program.

At one point during the study period, Carter acknowledged that he might be open to wholesale upgrading of discharges for those who were "alcoholics and persons who were too mentally incompetent to complete the basic training." I suggested in a magazine article at the time, "What the President will discover if he examines more cases is that virtually all persons fall into some category that most Americans would probably agree does not deserve the lifetime stigma these discharges represent."

I don't know if Carter ever read the testimony of some veterans' group leaders like Donald Schwab, legislative director for the Veterans of Foreign Wars (VFW), who told a House committee in 1976: "Congress should require the Department of Defense to review on its own motion all less-than-honorable discharges as a result of a misdemeanor and upgrade them to make them veterans in fact and entitled to the full range of veterans benefits." He was referring to the thousands who got undesirable discharges for offenses like "failure to pay debts," "inaptitude," "homosexual tendencies," and "unsanitary habits."

The Clemency Board had considered only 20,000 cases in its year of operation, although the Military Discharge Review Boards heard about 10,000 cases each year. Since 425,000 people were theoretically eligible for consideration, at this rate the process would take twenty years to complete. Of course, the Boards knew that all would not apply. Many ended up in prisons because their discharge status foreclosed the jobs that they needed to feed their families, while others were in prisons or mental institutions for drug use or psychological trauma acquired during their military service. Others were simply turned off by the bureaucratic disinterest in them once they left the military.

Senators James Abourezk (D/SD) and Ed Brooke (R/MA) were offended by the difficulty of getting these "bad paper" discharges reviewed and possibly upgraded to "general" discharges. They wrote a bill that would significantly streamline the process of discharge review for Vietnam veterans. They wanted to include it in that year's defense authorization bill. Senator Bob Dole (R/KS) objected to this, and negotiations began.

The Senators needed to buy more time for their negotiations, so they used a procedural tactic to do so. A single Senator could go to the presiding officer of the Senate and place a one day hold on proceeding to consideration of the defense bill. On alternating days, Abourezk or Brooke would put a hold on the legislation causing the whole bill to languish. I generally spoke to Abourezk every afternoon while I worked on getting support from other Senators, including Senator Alan Cranston (D/CA), who initially had some issues with the bill. One Thursday in August Abourezk asked if I had gotten as much support and the best language we were likely to get. Yes, I had. He said he'd tell Brooke and they'd just take their holds off the bill.

I told the Senator I'd be going on a vacation the next day and gave him the phone number of the Ocean City hotel where I'd be staying. Shortly after my arrival, the phone rang and Abourezk said, "So, we took our holds off, but Dole thought something suspicious was going on and put a hold on." He continued that Dole wanted an expansion of the bill to provide streamlined procedures not only to Vietnam veterans but those who served in any war. That made perfectly good sense to me, and, the committee agreeing, the bill quickly moved to the floor and was approved.

I was glad this bill passed, but annoyed that few people who supported the amnesty movement played much of a role in getting it passed.

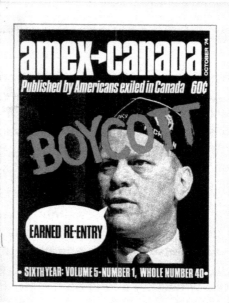

AmEx Canada was the most comprehensive resource about Vietnam war resistance. Source: Jack Calhoun and Steve Grossman

Washington Star-News

kl.. ₂₀₀   Copyright © 1974   WASHINGTON, D. C., SATURDAY, OCTOBER 26, 1974 —80 PAGES
Evening Star Newspaper Co.

OVER 5,000 FUGITIVES NAMED

U.S. Releases Draft-Evader List

By John Fialka
Star-News Staff Writer

The Department of Justice has released the names of more than 5,000 men who are under indictment for draft evasion during the 1964-73 Vietnam War period and are still fugitives.

The United Church of Christ and the American Civil Liberties Union announced yesterday, after the Justice Department released the list, that they will use it as a "tool" to counsel Vietnam-era draft resisters who still fear they may be prosecuted.

Rev. Barry Lynn, amnesty coordinator for the United Church of Christ, flipped through the list, an inch-thick computer printout, at a press conference. This is the list the Department of Justice claimed did not exist," he told reporters.

Rev. Lynn said his group had been pressing Justice for the list for several weeks under the Freedom of Information Act and had been told by some Justice lawyers that it had never been compiled. Yesterday, Asst. Atty. Gen. Henry Petersen released the list to the groups, accompanied by a letter saying that Justice could not vouch for its total accuracy and that it would have to be checked with Social Security Administration records for verification in each case.

Henry Schwarzschild, director of the ACLU amnesty project, noted that the list was relatively small compared to 206,775 men who were deemed draft evaders during the Vietnam War.

"A GREAT many thousands of men now think they are in legal jeopardy over the draft program," said Schwarzschild, asserting that many may have been hiding underground or exiled for years when, in fact, the Justice Department had decided not to prosecute.

As a result, the ACLU lawyer asserted, many young men who volunteer to accept the terms of President Ford's amnesty program represent cases that the Justice Department has dropped.

Schwarzschild said that an admission of guilt under such circumstances amounts to being "Shanghaied." He said that the ACLU and other volunteer groups will help potential applicants for the amnesty program determine the exact status of their cases before they go to a U.S. attorney's office.

Persons who are concerned about their cases, he said, could make collect calls to a national Clemency Information Center in Indianapolis, Ind., 317-635-8259. These in Canada may call the War Resister Information Program at a toll-free number, 800-665-8885.

Meanwhile, the Defense Department announced that it had processed 1,481 war deserters through its phase of the amnesty program, which offers a clemency discharge if an applicant volunteers to spend up to two years performing alternate public service.

OF THESE, according to a spokesman for the Selective Service, which administers the public service program, 826 have registered with their local draft boards but only 41 have found acceptable jobs.

The spokesman explained that those who accept the amnesty terms have up to 30 days to hunt for jobs and that most of the deserters going through the program are new in the 30-day job hunting period. "In about a month from now we'll know where we stand," he added.

The Justice Department, which processes draft evaders under the amnesty program, said that only 66 men had accepted amnesty as of last Monday.

Chapter 5

AT THE UCC AFTER AMNESTY

Religious Organizations and Lobbying

My work for the United Church of Christ on the issue of amnesty was noted approvingly by the denomination's hierarchy. Rarely were other church officials interviewed on nightly news broadcasts or on shows like *60 Minutes.*

This official denominational approval and my ability to give reporters what they wanted—a 15-second comment or a 22-second one—earned me widespread ecumenical support as well. When the amnesty and veterans' discharge activity had achieved what I thought was the optimal result achievable within the political reality of the time, my internship was over.

Paul Kittlaus and his boss, Larold K. Schultz, were fans of mine, though, and they were eager to find a way to continue to employ me at the agency, now called the Office for Church in Society. I told them I was eager to stay and suggested I work on a broader range of civil liberties and criminal justice issues. I had passed the bar examination for the District of Columbia, which gave me a little more cachet in speaking on these topics.

In Washington in the late 1970s, most religious entities were still located at 100-110 Maryland Avenue NE, the so-called Washington "God Box." This building also housed a few secular non-profits and served as the residence for several members of Congress, including Democratic Senator Sam Ervin, the self-named "country lawyer" who had effectively led the previous summer's Watergate hearings that exposed President Nixon's misconduct. Another tenant was Newt Gingrich, the ultraconservative Georgia Republican Congressman who later became Speaker of the House.

Washington religious groups in the late 1970s sponsored an entity called the Washington Interreligious Staff Council (WISC), which met once a week. When I first arrived, at those meetings staff could mention things that were of interest in the past two days' editions of *The Washington Post*. Little time was spent on developing strategies for having an effect on Congress. Many of the staff were uncomfortable with being considered lobbyists and saw their role primarily, if not exclusively, as reporting to their constituencies what Congress was doing. Policy advocacy mainly occurred through another coalition called IMPACT, which would issue occasional "action alerts" that took clear positions on proposed legislation, insulating some of the denominational offices from having to deal directly with the sausage-making process of Congress. On occasion, WISC would present testimony to Congress through a spokesperson from one office with the approval of other task force members. As the chair of the WISC Taskforce on Criminal Justice, I testified occasionally on issues such as alternatives to incarceration and opposition to capital punishment.

Few other staff for religious organizations had law degrees, so I became chief strategist of the coalitions of religious organizations addressing civil rights and civil liberties. I developed insider knowledge about how to present the views of non-governmental organizations (NGOs) on public policy to Congress and executive agencies. I was troubled by government funding projects with clear religious orientations. I was concerned even then about giving religious groups any benefits not available to secular groups.

One example was the effort to regulate lobbying. Congress during this period wanted, in theory, to clean up politics by insisting on the disclosure of activities by non-profits that were trying to influence legislation. Working with the American Civil Liberties Union, we developed a strategy for how to get Congress to take seriously the constitutional issues involved in regulating advocacy activities by non-profits.

The Office for Church in Society periodically published voting records of members of Congress, a table showing issues the denomination had taken a stand on and how each Member voted on each issue. In June of 1978, the Internal Revenue Service had issued a revenue ruling that indicated that certain forms of voting records constituted prohibited intervention in political campaigns for non-profit organizations. Prohibited were records that stated the position of the organization and then indicated with a symbol like a plus or minus sign whether the Member voted in accord with that position. This was the kind of voting record we published. The Internal Revenue Code states "All tax exempt 501(c)(3) organizations are absolutely prohibited from directly or indirectly participating in, or intervening in, any political campaign on behalf of (or in opposition to) any candidate for elective public office. Contributions to political campaign funds or public statements of position (verbal or written) made on behalf of the organization in favor of or in opposition to any candidate for public office clearly violate the prohibition against political campaign activity. Violating this prohibition may result in denial or revocation of tax-exempt status and the imposition of certain excise taxes."

In January 1979, the UCC, represented by the ACLU, argued that this revenue ruling, which had caused us to suspend publication of our voting records, was unconstitutional and should be revoked. Although some of what I said about voting records now seems hopelessly naïve, lobbying by non-profit religious groups was in its infancy, a kind of cottage industry rather than the monstrous machinery of groups that were soon to emerge, like the Christian Coalition and the Moral Majority. In challenging the ruling I said that the voting records were "simply a clear way for our subscribers to understand how Congresspeople responded to some of the crucial ethical issues of the day. Moral critique of government actions has always been an integral part of the ministry of American religious institutions."

I explained in a press release that the UCC had originally intended to publish a voting record in September of the previous year but suspended that action from the fear that non-compliance with the revenue ruling could lead to the loss of tax exemption for the entire

1.8-million-member denomination and many of its children's homes, medical facilities, and local churches. I concluded: "Although we could not take such a massive risk, our rights have been grossly violated. It is shocking that merely reporting public facts in an understandable form can create such an enormous threat to our very existence."

Legal counsel at the ACLU was an enormously talented man named David E. Landau. He argued that the government was under no obligation to grant tax exemptions, but that "once it decides to do so, it cannot impose conditions upon such exemptions which discourage or deter the free exercise of First Amendment rights." Landau also noted that a similar provision in the Federal Election Campaign Act had been declared unconstitutional in 1975. He indicated that if the revenue ruling was not withdrawn, the ACLU would seek relief on our behalf in the Federal District Court for the District of Columbia.

Landau felt that it was essential that I testify to the House Judiciary Committee about the problem that proposed legislation on "lobby disclosure" presented to small religious groups. This I did, along with Landau and a number of secular non-profits that expressed their objections to many of the proposals. My argument was that big lobbying groups, whether the American Medical Association, Lockheed, or Common Cause, would find lobbying regulations much easier to comply with than modest-sized groups which have no excess capital: "Lobbying disclosure represents an example of disparate effect on small organizations."

In a frontal assault on most of the proposed legislation, I argued that lobbying regulation impeded the "free exercise of religion" protected by the First Amendment, generated great practical difficulties for religious groups, and could be accomplished through other means.

The "free exercise of religion" argument I made then was much stronger than I would make it today. It was based on a number of Supreme Court cases at the time, including one where Amish parents refused to send their children to public high schools in Wisconsin. They prevailed and the opinion noted: "...only those interests of the highest order and those not otherwise served can overbalance legitimate claims to the free exercise of religion" and found no harm "to the public safety, peace, order, or welfare" in the refusal to send children to a public school. I analogized that requiring detailed disclosure of activities similarly was not going to protect safety, peace, order, or welfare and was therefore not a "highest order" justification for regulation.

A lobbying disclosure bill passed the House of Representatives in April 1978. It was intrusive when it got out of committee and became more so through floor amendments. Some of the top civil libertarians in Congress at the time opposed it strenuously, including California Democratic Congressman Don Edwards ("the worst legislation I have seen in my fifteen years in Congress") and Texas Democratic Congresswoman Barbara Jordan (the provisions "turn the Constitution on its head").

I told Congress that there were plenty of administrative costs connected to "lobby disclosure." The bill, as it passed out of the Judiciary Committee, required the registration of any organization that employs even a single person who spends any part of thirteen days per quarter in "lobbying communications," defined as "any oral or written communication with a member or staff person for a member or top executive branch officials with the intent of influencing legislation." The bill presumed that the expenditures of such a person will cross the $2500 manditory reporting threshold because salaries, mailings, telephone calls, and printing will all constitute expenditures. New enforcement policies would be put in place to catch miscreants who under-reported expenditures and all back-up records would have to be kept for five years.

Common Cause, the principal organization that supported expanding lobby disclosure, was unsatisfied with the legislation that came from the Committee and successfully added even more onerous provisions in floor amendments. Representative Walter Flowers (D/AL) successfully got one passed to cover "lobbying solicitations," any communications between an organization and its members or the public that urged contact with members of Congress on any specific issue. Compounding the burden, such communication required a copy of the promotion or a description of its contents if the organization expected it to be seen by at least 500 people. If an organization had affiliates or if a denomination had individual churches and it contacted twelve of them, such private communication would then become a matter of public record. Another amendment mandated the disclosure of the names of any group that contributed $3,000 to a registered organization and demanded that the CEO of such organization, even if unpaid herself, should disclose the precise issues about which the group lobbied. This prompted Andrew Feinstein of Ralph Nader's Congress Watch to lament that this was "the first step toward licensing the exercise of First Amendment rights."

Our opposition to this bill succeeded in defeating it. No lobbying disclosure bill passed both houses of Congress until 1995. That law was considerably more modest and had only limited impact on small non-profits.

Defending "Cults"

Then, an entirely different religious freedom issue arrived.

Bob Dole (R/KS) was an unsuccessful candidate for President in 1988 and 1996. I never understood why he didn't promote his extraordinary military career more fully in his campaigns. He had been seriously injured in World War II and had a limp and one nonfunctioning hand. He was also the third person to receive penicillin for a severe infection. The first person died; the second went blind; and Dole survived.

I had three powerful encounters with Dole. Widely known as a person who never forgot or forgave a slight, he never really forgave me for the first one. In 1979, a congressional delegation, led by Representative Leo Ryan (D/CA), went to Guyana to investigate the activities of a former California minister named Jim Jones. Jones had been ordained as a Disciples of Christ minister and was active in the San Francisco area putting together integrated worship and community services. He founded the Peoples' Temple and moved his activities to Guyana in 1977.

Controversy began shortly after his departure as family members began to suggest to elected officials, including Congressman Ryan, that they felt something was amiss there and that they were having trouble communicating with their loved ones.

Ryan, along with a few of his staff, including Jackie Speier (later a California Congresswoman who retired in 2023), went on a fact-finding mission to see what was happening, against the advice of the State Department under the Carter Administration and the Democratic Party establishment. They heard frightening stories of Jones' conduct and control over every aspect of the lives of his followers. As the congressional group was about to board a plane to leave one Sunday morning, its members were fired on by some of Jones' followers. Speier was shot five times and Congressman Ryan was killed, one of the only members of Congress to die in the line of official duty.

News of Ryan's assassination spread quickly, and members of the House and Senate formed a "special committee" led by liberal Democrat Joe Ottinger of New York and Senator Dole to focus on dangers from new religious movements. This whole effort did not sit well with me.

A few days before the scheduled hearing, I asked some of the religious leaders in the so-called Washington God Box whether they too were uncomfortable with this investigation. They were. So, I drafted a letter objecting to the premise of the hearing, suggesting that when Congress investigates any religion, no matter the strange nature of its practices or even allegations of possible criminal activity, it must do so carefully. The letter was signed by about a dozen religious leaders in just one day.

I sent the letter to Dole and Ottinger, but then decided it might get more notice if I also leaked it to *The Washington Post*. *The Post*'s story the next day was well placed, and Dole was particularly unhappy. His staff called me the morning it ran and suggested an afternoon meeting with the Senator's chief of staff to "see what could be done."

Late in the afternoon, I walked over to Dole's office and sat down for the meeting in a room right inside the main office door. The room's door was shut and the conversation began. After a few minutes, I noticed that there was a shadow moving across the floor outside that door, and I could hear footsteps of someone who seemed to be walking with a limp. It could only be Dole himself, eavesdropping on this meeting. Within a short time, his chief of staff said he was sure the Committee would love to hear about the Constitution and, since I was a lawyer, why didn't I testify? Many of the co-signers had already urged me to do so and I accepted the offer. I accepted loudly, and the shadow promptly disappeared. In the days following this encounter, the Committee also invited a few other advocates for a broad definition of religious freedom, as well as the President of the Unification Church in the United States, Neal Salonen.

The hearing was held the following week on the same day that a group of farmers, driving tractors, descended on Washington, demanding increased parity for their crops. This was part of a months-long effort to insist that changes were necessary to that year's omnibus farm bill to prevent their farms from going bankrupt. Dole was a supporter of that effort. The tractor caravan was disruptive of traffic, and when the tractors parked near the National Mall, they dug up a lot of grass and made a huge mess. Dole was embarrassed. The hearing did not go well for Dole, Ottinger, or any of the other members of Congress in attendance. The press took it as a subject for ridicule (despite the seriousness of Ryan's murder) and questions were raised about "grandstanding" by Dole.

At the hearing, I insisted that Congress tread lightly and said that courts repeatedly ruled that efforts to restrict religiously motivated activity would only succeed if the activity being restricted endangered paramount state interests. I criticized law professor Richard Delgado and others who "engage in an unsystematic chronicling of terrifying anecdotes and quasi-scientific reports which lead them to a theory of 'mind control' at least as dubious and incomprehensible as the theologies of the religious groups they attack." Despite the reference to odd theologies, the audience, which included a large number of Scientologists and members of the Unification Church, applauded that line wildly.

Several witnesses spoke about the dangers of what they characterized as "cults," with professional "deprogrammer" Ted Patrick explaining that cult members' "minds were like containers with the lids on tight; put them under the faucet and nothing can come in. What I've got to do in deprogramming is take the top off." The audience booed his testimony but reserved even more anger for Rabbi Maurice Davis of White Plains, New York, who compared the Unification Church to the Nazi Youth Movement and wrapped up his testimony with the inflammatory remark, "I am here to protest against child molesters. For as surely as there are those who lure children with lollipops in order to rape their bodies, so, too, do these lure children with candy-coated lies in order to rape their minds."

I urged the Committee, if it decided to do anything in response to new religious movements, to "err on the side of religious tolerance. When our nation's leaders have done otherwise...they have always plunged us into the darkest periods of our history." I concluded that one of the UCC's spiritual forbearers was the Congregational Church in Salem, Massachusetts, and a Congregational elder presided over the Salem witchcraft trials and "with that sense of history we are particularly troubled at any hint of governmental scrutiny of religious faith or beliefs."

The double whammy of the tractor fiasco and this hearing was not what Dole had planned as a backdrop to his imminent announcement of his presidential candidacy. He never forgot who caused this problem. The hearing itself was the end of this assault on religious freedom.

Bringing Back the Draft (Registration)–Round 1, 1979-1980

Conscription, forced military service, is perhaps the most immoral institution created by mankind, at least since chattel slavery. I was delighted when Richard Nixon ended the draft during the last period of the Vietnam War and was horrified when Jimmy Carter tried to start its return toward the end of his term as President. Along the way, drafting young men into the military was championed not only by militarist Republicans but also by the occasional liberal Democrat who mistakenly believed that it would somehow "equalize" service by making the military a place populated by persons of every race, creed, and economic background.

I felt guilty about being excluded from the pool of those to be conscripted and vowed I would do everything I could to aid those who ended up resisting the draft or getting seriously damaged by the military itself. After President Carter granted his partial "amnesty" and Senators Brooke and Abourezk got their military discharge review bill signed, I felt that I had done something useful.

But then came 1979 and serious talk about returning to conscription. Early that year Representative Charles E. Bennett, a Florida Democrat and second ranking member of the House Armed Services Committee, introduced legislation requiring the President to order the Selective Service System to start registering men by October 1. His bill would also have amended the Privacy Act to allow the Selective Service to gather personal data from high school graduation lists, drivers' license databases, and Social Security lists. The most vocal opponent of this legislation was Democratic Representative Jim Weaver of Oregon, who made it clear that this was a world-class terrible idea: "To require millions of our citizens to register with another federal agency, to then require them to carry a registration card at all times, to notify the government whenever they change their address, and to live with the constant threat of being uprooted and pressed into service would be a needless governmental intrusion that would not be balanced by any real increase in our security." The country would hear much about these arguments over the next eighteen months.

A similar registration bill was proposed in the Senate by Senators Harry Byrd (I/VA) and Sam Nunn (D/GA). It added the feature that if a President wanted to suspend registration (as Nixon had done), the suspension could be for no longer than ninety days and solely for the purpose of revising the technical procedures for conducting registration.

Other members of Congress wanted to modify the military draft by coming up with a program of national service. Representative John Cavanaugh (D/NE) proposed that all men register prior to their eighteenth birthday and choose whether to be considered for military or civilian service, with educational assistance tied only to military service.

Representative Paul N. "Pete" McCloskey (R/CA) had come up with an even more sweeping compulsory national service plan that required registration of all young people within ten days of their seventeenth birthday at which time they would receive counseling as to whether to volunteer for two years of military service with educational benefits or a single year of civilian service.

McCloskey was an interesting character. He had unsuccessfully challenged Richard Nixon for the Republican Presidential nomination in 1972 and supported an end to the war in Vietnam. I first met him when the head of the Northern California Conference of the United Church of Christ, the Reverend John Deckenback, invited me to debate McCloskey on the national service issue. It is actually quite rare for a member of Congress to agree to debate a member of the public, particularly one who doesn't reside in her or his district, so I was eager to go to California for this interchange. Another of these debates was on Maury Povich's talk show *Panorama* in Washington DC. The debate was followed by an interview with actress Lauren Bacall. As we were leaving the set, she came up to McCloskey. "I really like your idea," she said. Turning to me, she noted in her famous withering voice, "You, not so much." McCloskey and I debated frequently thereafter.

As all these ideas were festering, many anti-draft advocates wondered where President Carter would stand. The year earlier he had addressed a conference on defense policy in Memphis, Tennessee, where he noted that any future draft would be "substantially different" from the one in the Vietnam era, particularly highlighting the disparity between financially better-off men who could afford to go to college for years and those who could not. Carter posited a system where there would be a lottery to include persons "in college or working on a farm or relatively illiterate [who all] ought to be handled in the same exact way..."

Available evidence could support Carter if he decided to take the "registration only" step. His Secretary of the Army, Clifford L. Alexander, Jr., had been clear that he thought registration would be prudent, an "administrative measure of little personal inconvenience but with potential benefit to the nation" in speeding up mobilization in case of a "near calamity." I noted that Alexander later "clarified" his support by indicating that he only meant "improved mobilization capability." In addition, studies by the Defense Department, the Selective Service System, and several other non-military analysts suggested that registration had some mobilization advantages. Nevertheless, Carter's budget for 1980 included "only" $9.8 million dollars for Selective Service to improve data processing and nothing for actual registration.

Most of the discussion as 1979 began dealt solely with registration, although John C. Stennis (D/MS), chair of the Senate Armed Services Committee, spoke on the floor about the "failure" of the all-volunteer force and seemed prepared to move all the way to a reinstatement of the draft itself. His colleagues in the House like G.V. "Sonny" Montgomery (D/MS) and Charles Wilson (D/TX) also supported actual inductions into active duty or the "individual ready reserves." My opposition to this idea was rooted in pronouncements of the governing body of the United Church of Christ called the General Synod.

After all the work done to grant even the limited amnesty for Vietnam war resisters, I was appalled that Congress would even consider returning to registration, much less a draft in any way, shape, or form. I began to organize opposition to this within the religious community, testified against registration to the House Armed Services Committee, and in April became the chair of the newly formed Committee Against Registration and the Draft (CARD), a coalition of religious and secular organizations ranging from the liberal Americans for Democratic Action to the libertarian National Taxpayers Union. The Director was Duane Shank, a peace activist and non-registrant whom I had worked with during the amnesty effort. David Landau of the ACLU was the Vice-Chair.

My first testimony against draft registration came on February 15, 1979. I testified along with Landau before a generally hostile House Subcommittee on Military Personnel. I made points that I would continue to refine for the next two years, focusing on what I considered the bizarre assumptions upon which calls for draft registration rested: "Many Americans are frankly baffled about how a nation with 2.1 million active duty personnel, 800,000 people in the Reserves, over 300,000 persons in the Individual Ready Reserve, between 50,000-100,000 persons in the Delayed Entry Program, and a history of being able to recruit over 20,000 'actual volunteers' even during such an unpopular war as Vietnam can be said to be insufficiently prepared for any real emergency." I urged the subcommittee to start by candidly telling the public how Defense Department military strategists "calculate risks and arrive at personnel needs."

The public has a remarkable lack of understanding of how military personnel decisions are made and how military "strength" is assessed. If you asked the average person what the Individual Ready Reserve is, she or he would not have any idea. Even many veterans are not aware that most of them could be called up in the event of a national emergency for six years after their tour of active duty is completed. These persons have actual military training and experience and would be far more capable of military action than the average eighteen-year-old.

The reaction to my testimony was sharp and unpleasant. It was led by the Chair, "Sonny" Montgomery, Tennessee's Republican Robin Beard, and Alabama's Democrat Bill Nichols. They were particularly concerned about the patriotism of young people, which they seemed to equate with a willingness to be registered, the racial makeup of the current All Volunteer Force, the risk posed from the Soviet Union, and the quality of currently serving personnel. Frankly, the whole debate on these matters suffered from an ahistorical understanding of the Vietnam draft, a ridiculous conflation of patriotism with support of government policy, and just plain ideological stupidity. What follows is an example from a Congressional hearing.

Lynn: "I think the American people deserve more information as to why or how the Defense Department reaches the conclusion that merely because there are more tanks in the Warsaw Pact countries, that means that they, in fact, plan to invade Europe...I don't think the fact that...there may be sizably more troops or tanks or aircraft in the Warsaw Pact nations means that it's likely that there will be a European land war."

Rep. Nichols: "If you met a bully out in the alley and he had a baseball bat and a knife or a Saturday night special, wouldn't you be a little leery of him? Wouldn't you feel like maybe you ought to go back in the house and get you a little defense of your own?"

Lynn: "I'd be a little leery of him, but also I would like to make sure he was planning to use it and not just going to a costume party carrying those things."

Later I suggested to rightwing Congressman Larry Hogan (R/MD), when he asked why the Soviets were spending billions on weapons that could be used in Europe, "Why does the United States have a nuclear overkill capacity of five, six, or seven times what would be required to decimate all life in the Soviet Union, the United States, and virtually everywhere else?"

On the racial makeup of the All-Volunteer Army, Robin Beard noted that "... by 1980, 45% of the junior enlisted of the Army will be black." He wasn't clear why this troubled him, but I saw nothing in his historical voting patterns that suggested that he was an advocate of anything that would enhance minority education, or economic status. I think persons like Beard just realized that, during the Sixties and Seventies, many African Americans were strenuous opponents of bloated defense budgets and thought that even such actions as sending people to the moon were diverting resources from programs to benefit the disproportionately poor persons of color right here in Earth. Having more African Americans in the military might mean more resistance to foolhardy escapades abroad.

In April, I joined a group of other religious advocates at a White House meeting with Stuart Eizenstadt, Assistant to the President for Domestic Affairs and Policy. When we asked what President Carter thought about registration, Eizenstat called it "an open question"; the Administration did not have a timetable to decide its position. He conceded that the reorganizing Selective Service was "low priority" relative to reorganizing other agencies. We pointed out that a letter co-signed by a bipartisan group of thirty-nine House members had recently been released and sent to the President which opposed "the draft, compulsory non-military national service, and universal registration."

Eventually, the President decided to maintain his funding request for $9.8 million dollars, which would be used to modernize the field structure of the Selective Service and to improve computerization of data. This would not fund actual in-person registration. As talk at hearings continued to include additional funding for registration itself, the White House decided to oppose that funding vigorously. Carter's head of the Office of Management and Budget had told the Congress in July that "the Administration is opposed to registration." Similarly, Defense Secretary Harold Brown wrote a letter indicating that the Selective Service System needed modernization but that "immediate collection of names through registration" is not the way to proceed. The White House staff had prepared forms that identified congressional members' positions on issues. Anti-draft members of Congress and citizen activists including me used these "lobby forms" and shared our findings daily. The leaders of this effort in the House were liberal Democrats like James Weaver (D/OR), Bob Carr (D/MI), and Patricia Schroeder (D/CO), as well as conservative stalwarts like Ron Paul (R/TX) and James Sensenbrenner (R/WI).

Despite efforts to bottle up registration, the largely Deep South membership of the House Armed Services Committee voted on May 11 to add a registration requirement to the huge defense procurement bill in a last-minute tactic I called "very devious, very clever, and very cowardly. The Members were too scared to do it openly. Never in American history has the draft been changed in this absolutely unprecedented way." I noted that these pro-registration Congresspersons "are the same people who are horrified at the prospect of registering handguns but have no hesitation about registering people instead." I also noted that "more and more people are not buying the idea that registration is not part of conscription. People are not being registered for some ping-pong tournament."

The only remaining hurdle that might block floor consideration was the powerful Rules Committee, which sets the process for considering committee bills, including whether amendments will be allowed and how long the debate will last. Subcommittee Chair Richard White (D/TX) decided to merge registration with the "must pass" defense authorization bill. Members pointed out that it was hypocritical to claim that a program not even scheduled to begin for two years (until 1981) could be deemed a matter of national security. Congressman Carr announced that he was preparing hundreds of amendments to at least make any system fairer than it was during Vietnam. The Rules Committee adjourned for a few days after hearing this.

When it reconvened, Congressman Chris Dodd (D/CT) proposed tabling the bill unless the registration provision was removed, and Congressman White was so irritated when it looked like this proposal might prevail that he angrily left the room. However, the Chair that day was Florida's progressive Democrat Claude Pepper (who had been castigated with the moniker "Red" Pepper by rightwingers). He decided to oppose Dodd's motion, leading to a tie vote, which meant Dodd's motion failed. Pepper had told constituents that he would help kill registration but apparently had changed his mind.

Procedurally, Dodd's motion was given another chance on the floor shortly thereafter. The debate was spirited. White turned beet red and furious, sweating so much that his glasses nearly slid off his face. He demanded a roll call vote after the chair had initially declared that Dodd's motion had prevailed. On the roll call, Dodd lost, 219-158.

Congresswoman Schroeder and I held a press conference the day before the vote in the full House to challenge the facts and the logic that would be used the next day to justify registration. At that event I summarized the testimony I and others had delivered to the House Armed Services Committee.

On recruitment numbers, I told the press, the much heralded "failure" to meet personnel objectives in the fiscal year was misleading because the military strength was at 99.1% of the Defense manpower objective and had risen 10% over the previous year. The first tour re-enlistment rate was at an all-time high of 44.2%. I said that even I found these trends surprising because "we have half of the Congress, privately and publicly, continually and falsely denigrating the quality and integrity of the persons who choose to serve, labeling the Army 'full of lowlifes' or 'a place to go when nobody else wants you.' If the military wants to maintain its bloated, over two-million-person force, it needs to work harder to continue the retention of skilled older personnel, not draft young unskilled people." Also important was that the recruit class during the past fiscal year contained a higher percentage of high school graduates and a lower percentage of persons scoring in the lowest aptitude test category than at any time in the country's history, including during the Korean War and the Vietnam war draft.

I pointed out that the current Selective Service System projections showed adequate capacity to provide any needed draftees expeditiously: the first inductees within thirty days of mobilization and 650,000 within six months under a worst-case scenario. The Selective Service director at the time, Robert Shuck, had finally admitted that this scenario assumed that no one would actually volunteer for service. The soaring enlistment rates during every conflict in which the United States had participated undermined pro-registration arguments. They assumed that there would be no notice before a war began and anticipated that there would be a casualty rate ten times greater than in Vietnam. The Congressional Budget Office had developed a plan to register all twenty-year-old men through a data matching program within five days and deliver inductees five days earlier than the Selective Service System needed them.

I concluded at the press conference by explaining: "What reviving this first step to the restoration of the draft will actually do is guarantee that the military will never clean up mismanagement of human resources, never develop equitable and humane treatment of recruits, and never bother to define a reasonable mission for the military in the 1980s and beyond."

On September 12, 1979, the House voted 252-163 to accept Congresswoman Schroeder's amendment to the Pentagon's fiscal 1980 procurement bill to eliminate the registration requirement in the Armed Services Committee version. Earlier that afternoon, the House had also rejected an amendment (by a 268-114 vote) proposed by Congressman Beard to have congressional leaders appoint a twenty-four-member Commission to assess the combat readiness of the military and to consider ways to improve it. As the chair of CARD, I issued a statement that called the no-registration vote "a tremendous victory for the civil and human rights of young people, and a step in the direction of a peaceful future." CARD vowed to stop a similar proposal for registration that was still pending in the Senate.

Indeed, just days after the defeat in the House, Senator Sam Nunn was granted a request to hold a closed session of the Armed Services Committee to discuss his idea to revive draft registration. I called this a "shocking and totally irresponsible method of beginning debate on a proposal to register sixteen million young people for the draft." I argued that something this monumental "should be debated under the strictest scrutiny of the public and the press." An aide to Senator John Warner (R-VA) told me that "if the session had been open, we would have Soviet agents in the audience."

Registration language was included and passed on a 4-3 vote in the committee.

The full Committee voted a few days later. By a 12-5 vote, they sent the whole proposal to the floor. As with the closed session, this session was held in the late afternoon and missed mention on the evening news. By morning, the vote was ignored because of extensive coverage of the death of actor John Wayne. When it came to possible consideration on the floor, Senators Mark Hatfield (R/OR) and George McGovern (D/SD) vowed to conduct a filibuster against it and force the Senate to stay in session beyond its scheduled August vacation. Majority Leader Robert Byrd (D/WV) managed to avoid this by holding a separate vote on registration.

Years later when I was again working non-stop to avoid the return of military conscription and even registration for the Selective Service System, I worked closely with Oregon Senator Mark Hatfield. Hatfield had been in the Army in World War II and was scheduled to be among the first group of soldiers to attack in Japan. The atomic bombing of Hiroshima and Nagasaki made that land invasion unnecessary and perhaps saved his life. His recollections of this were a big part of his book, *Between A Rock and A Hard Place,* as he explored the moral questions around use of a nuclear weapon, its catastrophic effects, and what he claimed was the saving of the lives of thousands of Americans. His first speech on the Senate floor after his election (a big deal for any newly elected Senator) was about his opposition to the Vietnam War. He was convinced that without a draft, that war could not have continued for as long as it did.

The Washington Star ran a story on September 12, 1979, headlined: "Low-Key Lobby Drive May Have Stalled Push for Peacetime Registration for Draft" which quoted pro-registration supporters like Sonny Montgomery (D/MS) and Robin Beard (R/TN) as doubting they had the votes to restart draft registration. The article reported that I had decided in February to look in my files for the phone numbers of the groups we organized to promote amnesty. I told the reporter that without their advocacy we wouldn't have gotten one hundred votes against registration.

The Committee Against Registration and the Draft never developed a top-down strategy. Instead, hundreds of grassroots groups came up with innovative organizing efforts. The ACLU's David Landau said: "The spontaneous grassroots activity is staggering. Not only do we in Washington not direct people on what to do, we can barely keep up with what is happening around the country."

The extraordinary activist and organizer Duane Shank was CARD's Director. He put it this way in an interview with *The Washington Post*: "It turned out that getting money and people to fight draft registration is much easier than I anticipated because people react to it in an emotional kind of way."

One group in Columbia, Missouri, fired off letters to all sixteen-year-olds in the city to warn them of the impending registration. The group's letter pointed out that the proposal would only affect men who turned eighteen in 1981 and were thus too young to vote in the upcoming 1980 elections. A woman in Chicago took petitions into nursing homes and pressed the question: "Do you want your grandchildren to fight another war?"

Only one major national action took place against registration and that was on the steps of the Capitol on April 30. It featured Senator Mark Hatfield; my friend and author of *Born on the Fourth of July*, Ron Kovic; Congressmen Jim Weaver (D/OR) and Ron Dellums (D/CA); Nancy Ramsey of the Women's' International League for Peace and Freedom; and me. I was in no mood to mince my words: "For every young person to register and report his or her movements—or go to jail for five years—is a mechanism more suitable for a police state than a democracy."

Ron Kovic told the crowd of about 500 people that he planned to go to Congressman "Pete" McCloskey's office to have a "debate" with him on compulsory national service. The discussion turned into a shouting match with McCloskey's staff and about 100 of us at the rally. McCloskey eventually called the Capitol Police.

On Labor Day of 1980, I flew to Chicago to do a next-day taping of *The Phil Donahue Show*, without question the best television talk show in history. Phil had me and the Commander-in-Chief of the

Veterans of Foreign Wars, Howard Vander Clute, on the show to debate the matter. Each day Phil took on some engaging issue and the show was live in Chicago and one or two other cities—it aired days (or, in a few markets, weeks) after the taping. As a practical matter, this allowed my dedicated colleague Aida Bound to take phone calls right after it aired to get contact information for people who wanted to oppose draft registration and generate a sizeable mailing list.

Phil's audience was remarkably diverse, and he took great phone calls to incorporate into the debate on stage. That morning a woman called in who described herself as a "military wife" with one child living on an enlistee's $8,000 annual salary in a small two-bedroom apartment. She described how the family was watching its benefits "erode right from underneath us," forcing them to move frequently. She asked Vander Clute, "How can you possibly look at recruiting people with benefits just sliding away?" When I watched the tape of this show I was unpleasantly surprised that the haircut I had gotten a week before was so short that it made me look like a potential recruit with big ears sticking out. This may have been a factor in one hate mailer's conclusion that "it looks like you put your pantyhose on too tight."

I had another curious debate in mid-November 1980, at the august Yale Political Union. My side of the anti-registration argument was shared with Bertram Gross, a fine writer and professor of political science at Hunter College in New York City. The other side was represented by General J. Milnor Roberts, executive director of the Reserve Officers Association, and (a bit unbelievably) former anti-Vietnam war Senator Eugene J. McCarthy. McCarthy, along with Senator Robert Kennedy, had sought to wrest the Presidential nomination from Lyndon Johnson's vice president Hubert H. Humphrey in 1968. Tragically, Kennedy was assassinated and the momentum that was his slipped away from McCarthy. Humphrey lost to Richard Nixon mainly because he seemed too close to Johnson and because people foolishly believed Nixon's last minute announcement that he had an actual "secret plan" to end the war, which of course he did not. At the debate McCarthy used what I called the "best of a bad lot of ideas to justify conscription, [ideas] nevertheless still bad."

Although that debate was easily won by my side according to the poll taken at the end of the event, it was what happened before and after that I found most interesting. McCarthy and a few students had dinner together. He told a story I had never heard before about one of my favorite Senators, Phil Hart of Michigan. Democratic Senators were getting tired of Senator Sam Ervin of North Carolina, who was labeled the "constitutional scholar" for the party, but whose views were quite conservative. A number of them decided to anoint Hart as their alternate scholar, a role which he was not necessarily eager to play.

Colonel Phelps Jones, national security director of the Veterans of Foreign Wars, had come with General Roberts to the debate. He and I were going to be housed in a Yale dormitory, which was fine by me until I found that the room had previously had a cat in it. I was so allergic to cats that I couldn't stay there, and the students who had picked me up at the airport quickly found me a room in a hotel about a block away. I enjoyed the room and didn't think much about it until the next morning when I encountered Colonel Jones at the restaurant in the hotel. He came over and asked: "What did you think of the room"? I told him my room at the hotel was fine. "Hotel? I stayed in a dorm room and it was strange. I walked into the bathroom an hour ago and there were girls in it too." I made a satirical passing reference that this "sounded like something more dangerous than combat."

There was no draft registration funding by the end of 1979.

Bringing Back the Draft (Registration)—Round 2, 1980

By 1980, however, everything changed, and we had a much bigger fight on our hands. On January 22, the Associated Press reported that President Carter was "considering a proposal that he ask Congress to authorize a peacetime registration of draft-age youths." David Landau and I spent the next day trading phone calls because both of us had heard rumors that this pro-registration move would be announced that evening during Carter's "State of the Union" address to Congress.

Indeed, Landau eventually got a draft of the speech, which included a call to begin registration: "I will send legislation and budget proposals to the Congress next month so that we can begin registration and then meet mobilization needs rapidly if they arise."

Few details beyond this were included that night, with nothing on the contentious question of whether both young women and young men would be registered. In that 1980 State of Union address, President Carter discussed how he wanted to begin a resurrection of sorts for the Military Selective Service System, apparently convinced by Vietnam War architects Eugene Rostow and George Ball—coupled with comments of National Security Advisor Zbigniew Brzezinski— that registering young men for the draft would signal the Soviets that America would not be intimidated.

The Soviet Union had in fact entered Afghanistan in December 1979. Carter had said in the speech: "I hope that it will not be necessary to impose the draft. However, we must be prepared for that possibility." As the words were spoken, I watched the network cameras focus on the leading pro-draft Democratic Senator, Carter's fellow Georgian, Sam Nunn. Nunn literally appeared to be licking his lips like the Big Bad Wolf after blowing down the first pig's home.

The rest of the speech made clear that Carter was prepared to use force in the Persian Gulf to protect U.S. access to oil. He called this expanding the "defense perimeter."

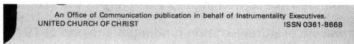

An Office of Communication publication in behalf of Instrumentality Executives.
UNITED CHURCH OF CHRIST   ISSN 0361-8668

OCIS' Barry Lynn addresses Capitol Hill rally last spring against draft registration.

Vol. 15, No. 2B, Feb. 15, 1980

Church Leaders Oppose Draft Registration Push

OCIS and UCBHM Issue Packet On 'Conscience and the Draft'

On the day of President Carter's State of the Union Address, top officials of denominations meeting in Cincinnati at the Consultation on Church Union issued a statement opposing the resumption of draft registration. [See next issue for an interpretation of COCU decisions from the UCC perspective.]

Reacting to reports that the President was considering reinstatement of Selective Service

Barry Lynn speaks to large anti-draft rally in Washington DC on March 23, 1980.

In that Presidential election year, many of the candidates competing for the job weighed in on the decision. Senator Edward Kennedy, thinking of challenging Carter for the Democratic nomination, said he was "unimpressed" and noted he was a longtime opponent of registration; Illinois Republican Congressman John Anderson called it "purely symbolic." California Democratic Governor Jerry Brown said it was "a serious error" that was edging closer "to getting bogged down in another Vietnam."

On the other side, Senator Howard Baker (R/TN) said it was "late" but that it "will have wide support in the Republican Party," while George H. W. Bush offered full support. Governor Ronald Reagan made no comment in response to Carter's speech that night, although he had been a longtime opponent of the draft and registration.

The day after the speech, I held another press conference with staunch anti-registration advocate Senator Mark Hatfield (R/OR) to give CARD's reaction and to elaborate on what the organization planned to do in the name of an "absolute commitment to prevent registration in the country" by organizing opposition "in every state of the Union." Having recruited the principal opposition inside and outside of Congress, an enormous amount of work lay ahead to wage a successful grassroots effort against this idea. The press strategy had to engage Selective Service officials everywhere possible. We had to select ways to reach Congress, making sure that David Landau and I, two white men, were supplemented by other people who could discuss specific aspects of the effort. Most significantly, we had to keep the liberal and conservative organizations on the same page. This all proved to be difficult, but a few factors increased our chances of success.

Bernard Rostker, was a thirty-five-year-old economist and defense manpower analyst for both the RAND Corporation and several branches of the military. He had volunteered for the Army in 1968, during the height of the Vietnam War. In November 1979, he became the Selective Service director. Rostker loved the publicity he gained from bringing a quiet little agency into the national spotlight.

During my press conference, I raised three major questions. First, if the registration was so crucial, why didn't the President use his current authority to start it immediately instead of going to Congress? Second, what had changed since the President opposed registration just a year previously? The Selective Service had the same mandate—first draftee in thirty days, 100,000 in six months and 650,000 in a year—all of which his administration had said could be achieved without registration. In 1979, the Defense Department had recruited 4,000 more volunteers for active duty than the year before, added almost 30,000 to the Ready Reserves, and welcomed another 20,000 to the Reserve and National Guard. The old pre-computer draft system during World Wars I and II managed to register 10 million and 14 million men in a single day. Finally, it seemed ludicrous that no comments had been made about the redeployment of troops in the Western Pacific or here at home, or increasing pay and benefits for recruits, thus backing ourselves into a return to the draft. I concluded that, just that morning in *The Washington Post*, an official at Selective Service said registration was "a vital step to gearing up for war." This comment alone summed up why draft registration could easily be seen as facilitating the return of conscription and foolhardy military intervention, perhaps to preserve access to oil.

Ironically, Rostker had for months thought it possible to register men only after a national emergency had been declared, drawing his evidence from those historic pre-computer registrations in World War I and World War II. Yet he knew that the prestigious Congressional Budget Office had concluded just two years earlier that pre-registering would only cut the induction time a scant thirteen days. Nevertheless, ignoring this information, Rostker went to the media the day after Carter's speech voicing that it was "the patriotic duty" of young people to sign up.

Anti-registration efforts began on college campuses within days, and the well-respected Central Committee for Conscientious Objectors revived its counseling program within a week. Anti-war activist Tom Hayden, arrested in Chicago during protests at the 1968 Democratic Convention in Chicago, and his wife, Jane Fonda, vowed to go to college campuses for a "campaign of resistance."

Much of the press coverage in the first few weeks was on the possibility of including women in the registration, with First Lady Rosalyn Carter and Secretary of the Army Clifford Alexander voicing support for including them. Phyllis Schlafly, of course, opposed this move as part of her continuing opposition to the Equal Rights Amendment and announced a petition drive to exempt women from registering. Then National Organization for Women president Ellie Smeal urged that neither women nor men should be registered. The ACLU had already agreed to file a lawsuit on behalf of a few men that a male-only registration would be unconstitutional. Notwithstanding Carter's embrace of the ERA and other feminist objectives, I never believed he would fight hard, if at all, for women to be registered. And he did not.

On January 31, 1980, Carter released his budget proposal, which included funding for registration and the removal of a section of the draft law that had been in place since 1972, which indicated that "no funds appropriated for the Selective Service System" could be "used for induction." He claimed the section was an unnecessary restriction on the President.

The President was also obliged to issue a report to Congress on February 9 about the need for registration. The press widely reported that the recommendation of the Selective Service System had been that registration would only be necessary in the event of a major wartime mobilization and that it could meet the mobilization needs of 100,000 inductees within two months and 650,000 in the first six. Thus, peacetime registration was unnecessary. Those responsible for this conclusion were allegedly instructed by the Administration to change the report. David Landau wrote a letter to Rostker demanding under the Freedom of Information Act to see "all files, documents, papers, reports, recommendations, and any drafts thereof, concerned with, averring to, or describing the Presidential study" required by Congress and gave him ten working days to respond. Senator Hatfield got the report and released it on February 25th.

By February with Carter's formal request for $21.9 million to begin registration in 1980 and a whopping $35.5 million for fiscal year 1981, anti-draft activists were mobilizing around the country with 3,000 people protesting in Los Angeles, 2,500 in New York and hundreds in places like Washington DC and Philadelphia. Carter's report called on Congress to include women: "a recognition of the reality that both women and men are working members of our society. It confirms what is already obvious throughout our society—that women are now providing all types of skills in every profession. The military should be no exception." Notwithstanding that obviously true statement, he noted that he would not be seeking any change to the current restriction on women serving in combat. His statement also urged that local draft boards be rebuilt so they too could be ready for immediate classification should inductions become necessary. When registration occurred later that year, it would only include the roughly four million persons born in 1960 or 1961. They would be eligible for induction until the age of twenty-six. In subsequent clarification, Stuart Eizenstat noted that registering people in other age groups would be "needlessly costly and cumbersome." Beginning in 1981, all men and women would be required to register when they turned eighteen. This was pure politics. It was what President Carter said he wanted.

MARK O. HATFIELD
OREGON

United States Senate
WASHINGTON, D.C.

April, 1980

Dear Friend:

Last year the Committee Against Registration and the Draft (CARD) did an excellent job of alerting the public to efforts being made to force draft registration on our young people. Their efforts were essential in building the practical, moral, and legal case against the return of draft registration. Last September the House of Representatives defeated registration by a nearly 100 vote margin.

This year, we will need CARD more than ever to block the President's new proposal for funding of registration in both the Senate and the House. Although world conditions have changed in the last six months there is still no need for draft registration to be imposed on young men and women. I do not want these young persons to have to face the grim choice of violating their conscience by registering for a system of military conscription or facing lengthy prison sentences. The only way to avoid forcing people to make that choice is to stop registration from being renewed.

Stopping registration will be a difficult, but far from impossible, task. I am convinced, however, that if we relax for even a moment, there will be a return to the draft. The efforts of the Committee Against Registration and the Draft will be critical in preventing this from happening.

Sincerely,

Mark O. Hatfield
United States Senator

MOH:rrj

Letter from Oregon Republican Senator Mark O. Hatfield thanking the Committee Against Registration and the Draft for its work derailing the revitalization of draft registration in 1979, urging more assistance to fight it again in 1980.

Congressional reaction on the registration of women was predictably mostly negative, with House Armed Services committee chair Richard White (D/TX) claiming (correctly I thought) that Carter "realizes that will not pass." Mark Hatfield (R/OR) said the plan would "deeply divide the country at exactly the time we need solidarity."

Congresswoman Patricia Shroeder (D/CO), who played such a large role in defeating registration in 1979, told *The Washington Post* that she was "a little ticked" when Carter changed his mind and was even angrier when a White House lobbyist told her: "Don't worry, you can carry the part about women." To which Schroeder said: "Are you kidding me? What a cheap shot. I'm not going to be used. I've never believed women should follow men into militarism. We came to Congress to make a difference...And we don't want to fight a war for a full tank of gas."

When Selective Service officials continued to clarify what registration would look like, people wanted to know how any draft that came after registration would be different from the draft of the Sixties. Selective Service official Brayton Harris said there would be no automatic deferments "for students, no occupational deferments and no automatic deferments for family status, including having children." Automatic deferments would only apply to "ministers of religion." Hardship and conscientious objection claims would be evaluated on a case-by-case basis.

By mid-February, every editorial board and syndicated columnist seemed to have an opinion on registration. My friend Mary McGrory, then a columnist for *The Washington Star*, called the registration push a "a gross overreaction." Some commented that since Carter had opposed registration just a few months earlier and now insisted it was vital to national security, it would seem foolish not to believe that he could move on to restore the draft without much additional provocation.

Also, by mid-February, there were rumors that, because Carter had not yet signed an order to begin registration, as he had indicated he would do, the White House was getting cold feet on forcing Congress to act before the election. I found that rumor unpersuasive, although many Democrats and Republicans in Congress did not. "The lemmings have not leaped from the cliff to the sea," I told the press. (Years later, I learned that lemmings do not jump to their deaths and that this belief grew almost entirely from depictions of a jump in a Disney movie, *White Wilderness*, where the production crew scared the creatures into jumping.)

By this time, Patrick Lacefield of the National Mobilization Against the Draft was organizing a massive demonstration in Washington on March 23. He told *The New York Times* that he expected thousands of people to show up to stop registration.

Carter held a meeting at the White House on February 15 to do a sales pitch to 300 student leaders about registration. Although reaction after the event was mixed, many students were ticked off that national security adviser Zbigniew Brzezinski conducted an exercise with them early in the day in which he asked, "How many of you are in favor of the volunteer Army?" Most raised their hands. As a follow up, he asked, "How many of you would volunteer?" Only a few hands remained up. As *The Baltimore Sun* reported, Brzezinski then snapped, "That's why we need registration" and "stalked out of the room." I and many others had grown tired of hearing such displays of arrogance from him and other architects of the war in Vietnam.

Congressional opposition arose early from Members like Tom Harkin (D/IA), who rose to fame for exposing the notorious Tiger Cages in Vietnam; William Clay (D/MO); Peter Kostmayer (D/PA); and my neighbor, Bob Carr (D/MI). They hoped that no bill that funded registration at the levels Carter proposed—starting at $20.5 million in the next fiscal year and including the registration of women—would hit the floor but were prepared with all kinds of amendments to point out some of the silliness and dangers of registration, should that occur. Some included registering only the "boat people" who had arrived from Cuba and draft quotas for members of the Church of Scientology and Rev. Sun Moon's Unification Church. Some insisted that Members who voted to fund registration be required to eat lunches together in the House cafeteria.

In the Senate, an interesting combination of opponents had come together. Senator Mark Hatfield of Oregon denounced the "hysterical voices" calling for a registration that would "threaten to hold hostage the freedom of millions of young men and provide a limitless manpower pool for any president willing to send American boys half a world away to fight in yet another war." Those sentiments were echoed by conservatives like Bill Armstrong (R/CO) and former Presidential candidate George McGovern (D/SD).

Early on, one poll showed that 70% of college students supported registration, seeming to consider it unconnected to actually being inducted into the military. This and other purported data led Carter's press secretary Jody Powell to issue a statement that the administration did not anticipate any serious opposition to draft registration. Within a day of the announcement, there were protests outside the White House and around the country with arrests occurring in Pittsburgh, Pennsylvania, and announcements from registration-age men all over the country that they would refuse to comply.

On February 25, Senator Hatfield released a report to the press containing the opposition arguments from the Director of Selective Service, prepared a week before Carter's announcement. Director Rostker said in the report that post-mobilization registration was preferred and would be "by far the most cost effective, and least intrusive, and is the option chosen by Selective Service." He had opposed registration in that report, erroneously assuming that Carter would continue his opposition. His confidential report had concluded that registering before a need to mobilize would only save seven days and that post-mobilization registration would still produce the first draftee in 17 days and 650,000 in 117 days, earlier than the Defense Department claimed to need new recruits. This internal document also claimed a male-only registration would be "legally suspect." Hatfield summarized: "The White House has either decided to bury or ignore the truth about registration. The truth is that the freedoms of millions of young men and women are being sacrificed for nothing more than a symbolic gesture."

After Hatfield released the report, White House press secretary Jody Powell said the President simply disagreed with the conclusions but offered no explanation of whose opinion he had accepted to justify that rejection.

The House Appropriations Subcommittee on Housing and Urban Development and Independent Agencies held a hearing on February 26 with virtually no notice, at which I testified again, along with my colleague David Landau. The next day, at the request of the White House, the subcommittee held a meeting to discuss the appropriation for Selective Service, authorizing $4.7 million for the service to upgrade computer facilities and planning capabilities. By a vote of 6-6, it did not authorize additional funds for registration. The Chair voted to register, in order to have the whole appropriations bill move to the full committee but argued that the failure of American allies to do much about a threat to oil reserves and the already-crumbling Russian position in Afghanistan made registration less important. Republicans on the Committee like Lawrence Coughlin of Pennsylvania called it a "useless gesture sending the wrong signal to the American people that we are doing something when we are not." Democrat Bob Traxler of Michigan ridiculed the idea that this was sending a signal to the Soviets. He questioned "whether this whimper can be heard beyond this room, to say nothing of overseas." Unhappy at the vote, House Democratic Majority Leader Jim Wright of Texas vowed to help Jamie Whitten (D/MS), chair of the full Appropriations Committee, to reverse the vote so that "the President not be denied or embarrassed."

The entire House Appropriations Committee was invited to a White House briefing on registration and heard from Secretary of Defense Harold Brown and other military officials who promoted the Carter plan calling it "an important and immediate" sign of "national resolve." Members of the committee had been expressing considerable doubts for weeks and were appalled at Majority Leader Wright's dedication to pushing through the funding so that the country wouldn't look "vacillating and undecided." Congresswoman Schroeder declared this approach was "amounting to saying, 'If the Commander-in-Chief says eat your foot, eat your foot.' Don't confuse the situation with the facts."

Shortly after the White House briefing, the Congressional Budget Office announced that Congress had gone $10 billion over the $547.6 billion spending ceiling from the past budget resolution and that no more funds could be appropriated unless the ceiling was raised, or other cuts were made. This led to a delay in the registration funding decision, although the personnel committee with only fifteen minutes discussion did vote 8-1 to eliminate women from the registration requirement. The White House began looking at the possibility of transferring funds from other programs to the Selective Service to avoid having to raise the debt ceiling. It ordered its lobbyists from all other agencies to contact friendly Members to support registration. *The Washington Post* quoted an anonymous administration official as saying: "We've done this kind of thing before, but we save it for the big ones."

With no solution to the debt ceiling complication, the Senate moved slowly on the issue. At a hearing in the Senate Appropriations Subcommittee on Independent Agencies, Senator Hatfield presented powerful testimony and the Lynn/Landau team testified again. I argued: "It is dangerously naïve for Congress and the Administration to believe that draft registration will be accepted by all young people. History documents that significant levels of non-cooperation will occur—followed by certain prosecutorial abuses and massive government surveillance of anti-draft activity....The Administration has tried to sell registration by saying that its rejection would be seen as a 'sign' of weakness. We believe that for this committee to reject the funding request would be a sign of both fiscal responsibility and a rational examination of the real issues." Although we did not mention this at the hearing, there were break-ins at the homes of David and me as well as Duane Shank, a weird set of occurrences that even prompted the head of the Justice Department's Civil Rights Division to discuss the matter with the three of us over lunch.

Anti-draft forces continued their agitation and lobbying. A major teach-in occurred in mid-March at the University of Michigan, complete with a standing ovation address by former Attorney General Ramsey Clark. Workshops were well-attended, including an early morning one with Congressman Bob Carr, who spoke to about forty attendees. Undaunted by what some saw as a weak turnout, Carr said, "It's hard to engage in anticipatory politics. It's a gradual process, not like turning on a light switch."

Anti-draft advocates had to keep tabs on wildly differing statistical claims about the quality of the all-volunteer force (AVF) and the rate of voluntary enlistment. A report on March 20 showed that 33,000 more people had enlisted in the first five months of fiscal 1980 than had in the previous year.

Saturday, March 23, 1980, was the day for the Washington, DC, protest march against registration that Lacefield had initiated. This event had been planned only a few months earlier and still drew about 30,000 people on a day with a fierce wind and temperatures much colder than expected in mid-March in Washington. It featured speakers from past anti-war activities like lifelong pacifist David Dellinger, African American rights advocate Kwame Ture (Stokely Carmichael), and Michael Harrington of the Democratic Socialists of America. A newer generation of activists, including Tom Palmer of Students for A Libertarian Society and Jeannie Martinelli, also spoke. Finally, a few of us (including myself) with a foot in both eras addressed the crowd. I said, "We are told that registration is a sign of national resolve to Soviets. I can't imagine any Soviet official losing any sleep over the collection of millions of names. The only people losing sleep, with grim justification, are millions of 18-, 19- and 20-year-old Americans."

This was the day I brought my three-year-old daughter to the speaker's podium on the Capitol steps and indicated that she was one of the millions of reasons I opposed registration, the draft to come, and the wars it would make easier. She was wearing a shirt that read: "Heck No, I Won't Go," which made her a popular photography model (including on this book's cover). Although she was happy that day and still loves to look at the pictures of her in my arms, I didn't feel right about her being a kind of prop for my work. She joined me later at rallies and speeches, but I never again brought her to the stage with me.

In a curious sidebar to the rally, members of the Rev. Sun Myung Moon's Unification Church attempted to disrupt several speakers, including me. They shouted that a draft would prevent future wars; about a dozen even rushed the platform but were blocked by volunteer marshals who formed a human barrier. A few days later I wrote to Neal Salonen, the church's President, calling his members' conduct "reprehensible and totally inconsistent with the free exchange of ideas which are so central in a democratic society." The UPI story on my letter noted that "in the past Mr. Lynn has been a staunch supporter of the First Amendment rights of the Unification Church." Salonen never responded.

David Landau and I wrote a letter to the Director of the Census regarding a comment by John White, deputy director of the Office of Management and Budget, that the administration was willing to use census data to find non-registrants. I alleged that this would violate federal law and urged the Census chief to repudiate White's comment immediately. I got a letter a few weeks later from Vincent Barabba, Director of the Census, assuring me that the way the census is conducted means "the Census data cannot be used to identify particular individuals."

I told *The New York Times*: "The President will find it was much easier to convince the Senate to fund registration than it will be to get nineteen- and twenty-year-olds to submit to draft registration." This became the Quote of the Day.

A few days after the rally, Congressman Robert W. Kastenmeier (D/WI) held a press conference to announce that his House Judiciary Subcommittee on Courts and Civil Liberties would hold a hearing on the problems of enforcing registration. He also released a study by the former regional counsel for Selective Service, Donald Gurwitz, that concluded that, because of the Vietnam experience and Supreme Court decisions liberalizing the definition of conscientious objection (CO), the country could "reasonably expect" that 50% of those sent induction notices would claim CO status. In the writer's view, the CO classification should be abolished or at least limited to pacifist religious sects, local draft boards should not have to give a reason for denying CO status, and the federal courts could not review a local board denial. Gurwitz considered but did not support a heavy tax on those who got CO status, which could have been enough to confiscate all funds that a CO obtained in excess of $5,000 for anywhere from five to twenty years.

Kastenmeier held that hearing on May 22. It was a serious undertaking, looking to examine the implications of draft registration for civil liberties and the judicial system. I focused on claims that 98% of young men would register, which I called "fantasy." I presented statistics that showed that in the last few years of the Vietnam Era 10%

111

of men did not register at all, while many others registered late or did not notify Selective Service when they moved. During this time there had been no inductions but the requirement to register remained in place. I also looked at the level of non-registration prosecutions and found them low (856 referrals by Selective Service to Justice in 1972 and 3,492 in 1973), and, strangely, neither agency could explain what happened to these cases.

In discussing the timing of registration, I indicated my belief that summer registration deliberately avoided turmoil at the Democratic National Convention or on America's college campuses and that part of the publicity campaign that Selective Service was promising had better include "printing maps of how to get to the post offices in Atlantic City and Daytona Beach" for the mobile population of teenagers in the summer. I also explained various legal issues, including the impropriety of matching data of the Selective Service with data of agencies like the IRS, the Social Security Administration, and the Census.

I concluded that "if registration occurs in July, there are 3.8 million men out there who are supposed to trudge off to the post office. Frankly, I do not think you could get nearly 4 million men in peacetime to register for a symbolic charade if you promised to give them a gold brick when they did it." (That too became a Quote of the Day in *The Times*.)

During the question period, I was asked if I thought any current draft would be more equitable, as Rostker had testified earlier at the hearing. My response was that Rostker might believe that, but I found it ridiculous because "when you have the first exemption or exception or deferment," you build in ways to game the system.

A meeting of the full House Appropriations Committee had been scheduled for the next day regarding paying for registration by transferring funds from the Air Force personnel budget, but the Chair had told House Speaker O'Neill that such a transfer could set a bad example. I speculated that there probably weren't enough votes to pass it out of committee.

Since the first test was a vote in the House of Representatives, we needed to have congressional opposition mirror to some degree the diversity of our coalition. The key Members were Libertarian Republican Ron Paul, a Texas physician who went home to his district on weekends to see patients, and, once again, Colorado Democrat Patricia Schroeder. The pair and their allies worked incredibly hard and met with me virtually every day, late in the afternoon, to share vote lists of opponents.

Ron Paul once told me how he had gotten an unbelievably conservative Georgia Republican, Larry McDonald, to oppose the registration under the theory that, since conservatives didn't want "your money to be taken away from you, you sure shouldn't want your children taken away either." McDonald eventually voted for registration anyway. Ron Paul pointed out that even the editors of the rabidly conservative John Birch Society publication opposed conscription. Pat Schroeder's most vigorous objection was that having an almost endless pool of potential draftees would encourage more military adventurism.

As members of the House went home for their Easter "district work period," I suggested that anti-draft activists visit them repeatedly to express their views and consider sit-ins if Members were not prepared to listen and discuss the issue. This comment upset Congressman Carr so much that he called me to express his belief that sit-ins could backfire.

When they returned to DC, an April 17 vote in the House Appropriations Committee transferred the Air Force funds to Selective Service on a 26-23 vote. The very next week, the full House held five hours of debate on registration.

The debate on the floor was intense. Many Republicans articulated their objections. Rep. Silvio Conte (R/MA) noted that "it is a tough decision to oppose the President on this issue...what I have concluded after examining the evidence is that pre-mobilization registration is a meaningless gesture..." His colleague Rep. Bob Michel (R/IL) was even more blunt: "If the President believes the Soviet rulers, shrewd men that they are, are going to be frightened by a wall of computer cards, he is mistaken once more."

Democrats then in opposition got straight to the point with Parren Mitchell (D/MD) claiming: "All we are doing in this resolution is preparing for a draft. Do not kid yourself. I do not care what the President says. I do not care what the Congress says. If we register people, we are going to draft them..."

There were unsuccessful efforts to add amendments to include women in the registration (defeated by voice vote); to move immediately to classification and examination of all men aged 18-26 (defeated 363-45); and to make registration "voluntary," Congressman Weaver's proposal (defeated 319-84).

The full House voted on this bill on April 22. After a robust debate, it passed, 218-188. This was considerably closer than the White House prediction that it would prevail by 50 to 100 votes.

Action then moved to the Senate, where a perfunctory "special hearing" had been held on the matter on March 11, at which I testified along with David Landau. Nobody asked a single question of either of us at that Appropriations Committee session. Within a few days, that Committee voted 17-9 to fund registration following hours of discussion by Senator Hatfield, who objected. He read letters from Carter's three major challengers for the Presidency (Senator Ted Kennedy, Governor Ronald Reagan, and Rep. John B. Anderson of Illinois, running as an independent) and reported on a phone call he had received from former President Gerald R. Ford. All of them urged rejection of registration funds. Hatfield also indicated that he had as many as thirty Senators prepared to remove registration when the bill hit the floor and believed he could convince many of the twenty-five "uncommitted" Senators to follow suit.

The Senate Appropriations Committee adopted by a 13-11 vote a Hatfield amendment that would require the registration form to contain a place for persons to declare themselves conscientious objectors. The Committee rejected his other amendment that had deleted funding for the selection and training of local draft boards. Literally one day later, it was disclosed that Selective Service had already printed twenty-five million registration forms, which seemed an arrogant presumption that Congress would pass registration.

Hatfield had a playful side. When I had my first meeting with him about opposing the return of military conscription, he was sitting in a large office area reading a newspaper in a position that blocked his face. Within a few minutes he lowered the paper and said "hello." He knew that any success in this effort in the Senate required support from some of its most conservative members, and he wanted to work hard to make that happen. One day I got a call from his staff about "good news." Bob Dole wanted to oppose draft registration, and would I join him and Hatfield to do a press conference? Of course I would.

About an hour later Hatfield's legislative director called back, asking, "What did you ever do to piss off Senator Dole? Dole will only do this press conference if you and he are not in the same camera shot." I told him about my actions to complicate Dole's anti-cult hearing.

On June 4, Senator Hatfield, Senator Bob Dole, and I held a press conference to announce his upcoming filibuster efforts, while I announced that there would be an anti-registration vigil on the steps of the Capitol while the Senate debate was occurring. Dole's refusal to be in the same camera shot with me at this well-attended event made it a bit awkward. I had to leave the bank of microphones any time Senator Dole wanted to respond to a question and Dole backed away whenever I spoke.

On June 12, the whole Senate approved the full funding of registration on a 58-34 vote. Hatfield's attempt to filibuster the measure, which required a vote to close debate, eventually led to a 61-32 vote and ended the filibuster. On the floor the conscientious objector amendment was defeated, in large part because of the Selective Service's pre-emptive printing of the forms; if conscientious objectors could identify themselves, the forms would have to be changed.

This version of the bill had a slight difference from the House bill, which meant that the House and Senate needed to vote one more time, after reconciling the two versions. This gave us one more chance to try to alter some House votes in support. I was on Larry King's late night talk show for two hours to make that point.

It was a strange night. The driver of the car that was supposed to pick me up for my 3 a.m. slot fell asleep in my neighbor's driveway. Once out of his stupor, he drove rapidly to King's studio in nearby Arlington, Virginia. As I started to explain my case, word came of the eruption of the Mount St. Helen's volcano in Washington State, so updates on this calamity were interspersed with my analysis.

The House voted again on June 25 and again approved registration, 234-168. Members could not bring themselves to vote differently on registration funds than they had earlier, and voting to stop the whole bill could be used by political opponents to show that they were "soft" on defense. During that final debate, Rep. Ron Paul (R/TX) noted that many members of the House who supported registration vehemently opposed registration of guns. "They think less of their kids than their guns," he said. Carter signed the bill authorizing registration on June 27, 1980.

Bringing Back the Draft (Registration)—Round 3, Late 1980

Many of us reminded the press that Carter had predicated registration on a need to appear strong to our enemies, including the Soviets, announcing his "Carter Doctrine" that "An attempt by any outside force to gain control of the Persian Gulf region will be regarded as an assault on the vital interests of the United States. It will be repelled by use of any means necessary, including the use of force."

Carter reversed another position in late June by agreeing to a Senate-backed proposal to increase allowances and benefits for current military personnel. Nevertheless, Senator Nunn (D/GA) still claimed that the military was withholding data on the worsening condition of the volunteer force; he warned that a draft might be needed. Nunn's alleged expertise on military matters looked ludicrous later when the Soviet Union literally fell apart in 1991. It became clear that Soviet military personnel had little interest in protecting the "Motherland."

After all the handwringing over whether to register women, both houses of Congress rejected the idea. The ACLU announced on June 26 that it was filing a lawsuit to have registration declared unconstitutional because of the absence of women. Isabelle Katz Pinzler, head of the ACLU's Womens' Rights Project, announced that sixteen male plaintiffs were being represented to show that "the exclusion of women cannot be justified on the basis of anything closely and substantially related to an important government purpose." The ACLU's Executive Director Ira Glasser called the suit "now the best way to stop draft registration entirely," alleging that Congress would not change its mind on that issue and would simply reject the move to register anyone.

As all this was going on, CARD made plans for what to do if registration occurred as Carter planned. I spoke at a press conference detailing some of our plans, including demonstrations at "as many of the 34,000 post offices as possible." We released copies of our question and answer pamphlet about registration, samples of postcards that stated "I am registering against the draft" which would be delivered to the White House, and stickers reading, "I am registering under protest" that could be attached to the registration forms so long as they did not obscure any relevant personal information. We also made clear that, if registration happened, there would be an "Anti-Draft Week" in October and a national conference sometime after the President was inaugurated.

Carter obviously wanted his call for registration to be part of the Democratic Party platform, to be approved in August at the New York City convention. I had testified at the Platform Committee on June 13. My conventional arguments were these: "It is ludicrous to assert that registration will be a signal of national resolve and commitment. No compulsory program in which a government strips some of its most vulnerable citizens of their rights—and that's what the draft does—is a sign of anything but despotism and injustice." I also pointed out that a male-only registration "is an affront to the very principle of equality which this party has long espoused," and that rushing to register young people for Selective Service before college-age students were back on campuses where they could more easily organize to oppose the draft, was clearly politically motivated. The idea that young people would learn of their obligation to register through "thirty-second public service announcements on radio...is destined to be a fiasco," I told the Platform Committee.

Notwithstanding my comments, the Platform Committee rejected an effort to disapprove registration, although Kennedy supporters indicated that they were prepared to have a floor fight on this and other issues.

July brought the moment of truth: would draft registration be successful or would there be such a lack of interest or willingness to register that the government would be hard-pressed to call it a "success" with a straight face? In early July, *The New York Times* weighed in on registration, noting that Carter's decision to exempt women and all men over twenty-one was an "obvious calculation, in an election year, [and] proved the very opposite of the resolve the President vowed to show after the Soviet Union marched into Afghanistan...Washington is stuck now with a registration that has neither practical nor symbolic value. Even if dutifully obeyed, it is futile." The editorial concluded by recommending that "after registering at the post office, they ought to register again, at the Board of Elections."

One day after the *Times* editorial, the President spoke in the Cabinet Room, again declaring that he opposed a peacetime draft and distributing a question and answer sheet about registration. He claimed that, if registration was not successful, it would be seen as a sign that Americans are not prepared to defend their "vital interests."

At about this time, I got a telephone call from actor Henry Gibson, who was one of the comedians in Rowan and Martin's *Laugh-In* and the star of Robert Altman's film *Nashville*. He had recently done an anti-war poem/op-ed for *The Washington Post* and wondered if I would like to support his effort to have some of his Hollywood friends produce radio spots about draft registration. These could run on the same radio stations that would soon be running announcements by the Selective Service System. I was thrilled. Gibson reached out to many of his friends, including Lily Tomlin, Levar Burton, Henry Winkler, and Martin Sheen (whom he woke up in the middle of the night while Sheen was filming a movie in London). Gibson told reporters that he anticipated difficulty in getting the spots on the air.

Just after the Independence Day recess, the Selective Service ads started to surface, featuring soul singer Lou Rawls, U.S. Olympic hockey coach Herb Brooks, and Ken Michelman of CBS' hit basketball show *The White Shadow*. These were distributed to stations in all major radio and television markets.

I threatened that we would file complaints with the Federal Communications Commission demanding under the "Fairness Doctrine" that any local station that aired the government ads should air ours, because draft registration was just the kind of public controversy that those stations were obliged to examine from all sides. I sent letters to the heads of each major television network arguing against using the ads because they went beyond merely stating a legal obligation and made controversial assertions about the value and implications of registration. I wrote, "I do not approve of controversy, inaccuracy and political campaigning masquerading as public service announcements."

The government ads did not mention the severe penalties ($10,000 fines and five years in prison) for those who did not comply with registration. This "oversight" could lead to a defense of non-registrants to claim they had been inadequately informed of the consequences of failure to register. The ads included misleading statements about how registration would enhance military preparedness and that the rights of conscientious objectors would be preserved. I pointed out that the ads often contained the assertion that "the United States is not going back to the draft," in spite of support for doing just that from the Chairman of the Senate Armed Services Committee and the Chief of Naval Operations.

My other complaint, echoed shortly thereafter by the Congressional Black Caucus and the National Urban League, was "the difference between the television spots geared to white audiences and those geared toward black and Hispanic audiences. The announcements featuring white youth emphasize registering because it is 'the right thing to do', while those featuring minority youth are harsher in tone and message ('Registering will keep you out of trouble' and 'If you don't [register] you will be breaking the law')." These differences were at best, insensitive, at worst, racially stereotyped.

Maudine R. Cooper, the Acting Vice President of the Urban League, wrote to Rostker: "The commercial with the two Black men playing basketball is offensive because it reinforces a negative stereotype about Black men—that they spend all their time playing basketball, wasting their lives away, going nowhere. Language in it is abrasive with a subtle warning that registering may keep them out of trouble. But it's not clearly stated if this means out of trouble with Selective Service or off the streets."

Upon learning of my letters, Selective Service public affairs officer Joan Lamb labeled my complaint "groundless" and "just a ploy of the people who oppose draft registration." She also noted that Deputy Director Dr. James G. Bond, who was black, had a degree in psychology, and was extremely sensitive, "... would not have allowed them to go through if they were offensive or discriminatory." Nevertheless, both NBC and CBS refused to air some of the ads. Ms. Lamb insisted that, even with our efforts, there would be nearly total compliance over the two-week registration period. I scoffed at that, again pointing out to *The New York Times* that, in the period when peacetime draft registration was winding down, between 1973 and 1975, there was only 90% compliance. Even that percentage now would create an immediate pool of 400,000 felons.

On the Friday before registration was to begin, a three-judge panel in a federal court in Philadelphia ruled that the current registration plan was unconstitutional because women had been excluded. I was deliriously happy, but the joy was short-lived. One day later, Supreme Court Justice William Brennan overruled the lower court's voiding registration. He cited three reasons. First, it would leave the "military capacity to respond to emergencies remaining uncertain." Second, it would eliminate the usefulness of the registration as "an independent act of foreign policy significance." Third, it would vitiate the "considerable resources already expended." These legal maneuvers left many potential registrants confused about their obligation.

On June 25, 1981, the Supreme Court issued its decision on the merits, upholding registration of men only as constitutional. I had attended the oral argument of the case several months earlier and in the elevator was joined by Senator Sam Nunn, who told me, "Barry, if I saw you wearing a black robe, I'd be worried."

Actual registrations began at post offices on Monday, July 21, 1980, with twenty-year-olds designated to register on specific days during the first week depending on their last names and Friday a make-up day. A similar schedule was planned for nineteen-year-olds the following week. A large rally occurred in New York City the evening of July 21. I was the lead-off speaker, with dozens of other speakers and musicians (including one of my favorite blues guitarists, Dave Van Ronk, and Peter Yarrow of Peter, Paul and Mary). Almost every local newspaper covered registration, but most seemed surprised by the slow pace of registrants and the relatively light turnout of anti-draft activists. Typical headlines were "Dade youths trickle in to register for the draft" (*The Miami News*); "Some obey Uncle Sam, others protest" (*The Pittsburgh Post-Gazette*); and "Men Begin Registering Here Without Incident" *(The Knoxville News-Sentinel)*. Several dozen anti-draft protestors were arrested in Boston, Kansas City, and San Francisco for refusing to leave post offices where they had formed barricades or chained themselves to post office desks.

When the first week of registration was over, *The New York Times'* Richard Halloran concluded "neither the government nor anti-draft organizations nor, apparently, anyone else could say it was succeeding or failing." A Selective Service official told him that it would be sixty days after registration ended before an official tally could be known. I estimated but couldn't confirm that at least 20% of those who were supposed to register had not done so. Alex Reyes of the National Resistance Committee told Halloran that in Dorchester, Massachusetts, there were only two registrants and twenty talked to a counselor and "turned around" to go home at least temporarily without registering.

Ron Kovic reported that he was proud that his younger brother had refused to register. Selective Service Director Rostker told *The New York Times* that the agency was serious about enforcing the registration mandate: "This is not Mickey Mouse. This is not a game—it's not 'ha ha, catch me if you can'. A person who fails to register is a felon, make no mistake about it...The kid who throws down the gauntlet to the Government will be prosecuted." Speaking of Mickey Mouse, numerous registrants did register as "Mickey Mouse." Donald Duck and Karl Marx also registered in a timely manner.

Early August brought the results of an "adjusted" analysis of the mental abilities of military recruits: considerably more persons in so-called "Category IV," those who score between the 10th and 30th percentile in the qualifications test. The numbers were disturbing to many of us. The Army had previously reported 9% in that category; the new numbers showed 46%. Draft supporters pointed to these new numbers as evidence of the failure of the all-volunteer force. I, on the other hand, reminded the press that, during the draft in World War II, 21% were in Category IV and another 9% were in an even lower category from which no one was taken by the late Seventies. The same report concluded that "most of the low-scoring people are performing adequately."

That August also brought comments by Major General Maxwell Thurman, commander of the Army's recruitment, that "a quality, all-volunteer Army is definitely recruitable." He criticized the relatively low pay for recruits and the termination of the GI bill for educational support in 1976 as a "powerful depressant." He said that if the pay was increased to more than the current 84% of minimum wage and educational benefits were tied to military service, you would have a better Army than with a draft because "people are there because they want to be."

By mid-August, Senator Edward Kennedy was rising in delegate strength and decided to negotiate with President Carter and not take certain platform differences to the floor. Included in that category was the issue of draft registration, which Kennedy continued to consider to be a significant error. This was disappointing to many of us who had hoped to hear a vigorous debate on the convention floor.

The alternative was to create a paper organization called Democrats Against the Draft and see if we could get enough delegate signatures to put the name of someone into nomination for vice president who could raise the issue. This was done to mirror the successful effort four years earlier to nominate draft resister Fritz Efaw for Vice President. I called Patricia Simon a few days before the convention to see if she would be willing to be nominated, and after only a modest hesitation, she agreed. Her only son David had been killed in Vietnam only three weeks after his arrival and just two days before his twentieth birthday. She had told me that her first instinct was to go to Vietnam and work in a Quaker day care center, but that she needed to stay in the United States so she could raise her three daughters. She gave a lengthy interview to *The Washington Star* in which she concluded with her definition of patriotism: "It means watching what your government is doing with your name and with your children and with your money and it means questioning and demanding to be a participant in the government of the people, by the people and for the people." We got the necessary 334 signatures, as did African American LGBTQ activist Melvin Boozer.

When the Democratic convention planners learned that Simon and Boozer would be nominated, they were unhappy that these two controversial topics would be aired in primetime, so they moved the Vice-Presidential nominating speeches to the afternoon. When I "escorted" Pat to the stage, claiming to be her "security team," a Wisconsin elected official I had worked with in the past said: "See what you have done. Now Walter Mondale has to be nominated at a time he will not be seen." Actually, of course, the Democratic Party had made that choice themselves. Patricia was nominated by New York Congressman Ted Weiss and seconded by a draft-age student from Hampshire College, Ben Meskin. This event got little coverage, but all the speeches were powerful ones for the relatively few persons in the convention center and those watching on television on that August afternoon.

Life with Draft Registration—The Reagan Years

A coalition built between people with as disparate views as Libertarians and Communists (and there were many factions in each) was not easy to keep together. For example, *The Spotlight* was a neo-Nazi publication, which opposed draft registration. African American anti-fascist journalist William Worthy, who went to Cuba to report, was ostracized for years, and now wrote for a progressive Black newspaper in Baltimore, also opposed the registration. CARD had already committed to holding a national meeting to discuss strategy early in the tenure of the next President, who turned out to be allegedly anti-registration Ronald Reagan. The site was to be a predominantly Black college in Detroit, Wayne State University, in mid-February 1981. The Congressman representing that area, John Conyers, spoke; Erma Henderson, who was President of the Detroit City Council, spoke, as did someone from the staff of Congressman Ron Paul, who argued that the draft was anti-Biblical.

As usual when I spoke, I tried to lighten up some of the politics with statements like: "[Defense Secretary] Caspar Weinberger seems to think that it would be a very serious administrative problem to roll back registration. We say it's only four million pieces of paper. Let's lift the government hiring freeze and hire Bonzo [a chimpanzee that was in one of Reagan's best-known films] to do it. When Reagan concedes that registration has caused some unrest, that's a classic understatement. It would be like Noah telling the animals going into the ark that they're in for a little rain." I made it clear that the winds were blowing clearly in the direction of Reagan keeping the system he had criticized so clearly during the campaign.

Saturday's session was a disaster, filled with acrimonious debate about creating a "statement of principles." Even the far left was not united, with members of the Spartacist League, the Revolutionary Communist Party, and the Socialist Workers Party (SWP) spouting differing agendas. The Socialist Workers' Party had 200 people at the conference and were hell-bent on passing a resolution that called for "funding human needs" through a government jobs program. They wanted to throw Libertarians out of the coalition, since this idea was anathema to that political strain of activism. Resolutions were passed to endorse a labor-backed demonstration in late March in Harrisburg, Pennsylvania, the site of the Three Mile Island nuclear incident some months earlier, and to hold national actions in Washington and San Francisco on May 9 to focus on the draft and U.S. intervention in El Salvador.

I had been staying at the apartment of a Socialist friend of mine but was told near the end of Saturday that a more leftist group was planning to "seize" that fellow's apartment and that, to be safe, I should move to a Libertarian's apartment, which I did. I have no idea how real the threat was, but I just wanted to make one more effort to keep this fragile coalition somewhat together.

By Sunday, the SWP, most of whose members stayed around, passed a resolution calling for an "open steering committee" for CARD, since, as one speaker put it: "there is no such thing as excessive democracy." This did not go over well with many of the attendees. Angie Fa of the Democratic Socialist Organizing Committee and Jim Bristol, a non-registrant for World War II who now worked with the American Friends Service Committee, called the numbers in an "open" steering committee "unworkable." Bristol noted that the SWP would use such a structure to set up bogus groups as it had during Vietnam anti-war activities. A representative of the United Auto Workers called it "a floating crap game for anyone who sets up a banana stand." Unfortunately, SWP won the final vote 160-117, after nearly 80% of the attendees had gone home.

I had already decided to step down as chair of CARD, but I summed up the conference for *In These Times* this way: "Clearly grassroots activists moved toward a better sense of goals and principles and a unity based on specifics rather than an unwillingness to address issues like the 'poverty draft' and military intervention. However, a sectarian group has attempted to use this conference for its own purposes and to gain control of the entire anti-draft movement. They will not succeed." In my heart, I knew CARD would fall apart before much else happened.

Eventually, a new group formed called Draft Action, which focused more on legislative matters. I was its president and wrote my first fundraising letter for them. It was sent to about 2,000 members of anti-war mailing lists that had been contributed for a one-time use. The response rate was phenomenal by direct mail standards, coming in at about 20%. The average direct mail piece has a 1% positive response rate.

Reagan had a long track record of opposing the draft and even sent Senator Mark Hatfield a letter in 1980 with all kinds of practical objections and concluding that, "a draft or draft registration destroys the very values our society is committed to defending." Even the great Walter Cronkite, when reporting on anti-draft demonstrators along the route of the inaugural day parade, erroneously declared that an executive order had already been written to stop the registration process. *Newsweek* magazine also noted, in error, that Reagan was going to allow registration to "expire" by the end of 1981. Technically it requires a two-paragraph executive order to accomplish that.

Although Reagan repeated his opposition to registration during his first press conference, he became strangely quiet about it for months thereafter as he hyped up his support for the largest peacetime military buildup in history. This was very troubling to all of us. On behalf of CARD, I sent a letter to the President-elect urging him to end registration early in his tenure to fulfill his campaign promises: "If you do not inform the Carter Administration that you want it gone, this useless collection of millions of names and addresses will cost the American taxpayers $5 million, followed by needless social trauma, and law enforcement problems." He did not respond to that letter, and Selective Service chief Rostker gleefully told me there was "no chance Reagan would stop registration."

What Reagan inherited was a system that registered men born in 1962 and every man born after 1962 had to register within thirty days of his eighteenth birthday. Reagan's staff had presumably seen reports from the General Accounting Office, a Congressional watchdog over government fraud and waste, which characterized registration numbers from the Carter era as largely correct, but with some minor errors. This conclusion was reached by using statistical methodology that would have been laughed out of my freshman statistics class in college. First, the GAO conceded that Selective Service had underestimated the registrant pool by 2%, meaning that there were 96,000 more non-registrants. Second, a sampling of registration cards led GAO to conclude that 28,000 "registrants" did not know they had registered (no reason was given but I speculated that this could be the result of somnambulism, an amnesia epidemic, or astral projection). Third, about 9,500 names were "obviously fictitious or unverifiable." In that category fell numerous Mickey Mouses and Jesse Helmses. The Mouse in Anaheim, California, actually received a threatening letter regarding his "incomplete form." His surrogate parents wrote back to clarify that, if Selective Service had watched his old films, they would realize that he was fifty-two and had served, reminding the government that he was a "cartoon character." Finally, a full 55,000 registrants had given clearly erroneous addresses such as "Earth." Several months later, GAO had to admit that another 3% were missing because it had used outdated census data.

For most of 1981 the registration process bumped along in fits and starts with only 69% of those required to register doing so during the first quarter of the year. By mid-year, even Selective Service had conceded that there were hundreds of thousands of non-registrants, "probably not much over 700,000," according to Brayton Harris. Selective Service complained that it needed access to more databases to do a better job, seeking with various degrees of success to require that registrants give their Social Security number and even Internal Revenue Service data.

Uncertain about its access to these records, Selective Service tried two more strategies. First, it announced that names and birthdates of all registrants would be posted in local public buildings near the address on the registration form. I posed this possibility: "Imagine the gang down at the Oshkosh American Legion Hall spending an evening comparing the names of registrants posted to names in recent high school yearbooks and then doing their patriotic duty by sending the government names of men who were in those yearbooks but not on the registration rolls." Second, Selective Service purchased the names of 1.2 million men from a Long Island list broker, who charged only $17 per 1000 names, and sent a postcard to all of them reminding them of their duty to register and the dire consequences of failure to do so. My friend Shaun Perry, who then worked for the National Interreligious Service Board for Conscientious Objectors, found this to have a goal beyond simple notification: "Many people who didn't register think it is a warning notice, that they've been discovered. I'm sure Selective Service doesn't mind giving that impression."

Just one day before the anniversary of the start of registration, the Justice Department's Associate Attorney General, Rudy Giuliani (long before he became "America's Mayor" after the 9-11 attacks and then turned into a buffoonish sycophant for ex-President Donald Trump), sent 150 men real "warning letters" that they were suspected of non-registration. The results: 30 registered; 37 were undeliverable; 17 weren't going to register; 40 were delivered but did not result in any response; 26 apparently went missing. When I asked Selective Service what happened to them, no one could give me an answer. Alex Reyes, a Libertarian leader of the National Resistance Committee, told me, "Your chances of being prosecuted were 1 in 1,000...[N]ow ... your chances are 1 in 100,000."

On August 1, Rostker hung up his drafting shoes and moved to a private management firm. Reagan chose as his replacement Army

National Guard General Thomas K. Turnage, who had served in World War II and Korea and was assigned previously to study personnel issues at the Defense Department. Turnage's other claim to fame was serving on the Reserve Forces Policy Board, whose chair had testified to Congress that there should be an immediate return to conscription.

All measures of size and composition of the all-volunteer military showed dramatic changes: more volunteers for active duty; greater career re-enlistment, and "better quality" recruits—the same percentage of recruits scored in the least qualified category as during the Vietnam era draft. Although this sounded like success, Reagan's Defense Department wanted to increase the size of the military by 500,000 persons. No one expected, even with a military pay raise, that this could be accomplished without a draft. Reagan still claimed to oppose a draft and even said so to the 1981 graduates of West Point. Although Reagan didn't make any announcement about registration, the Defense Secretary told an interviewer in June that there were no plans to scrap registration and that he wanted to avoid scrapping the all-volunteer force (AVF) "as long as possible." Making the AVF disappear was unlikely in the 1982 election year and all politicians understood that.

As I feared, these ominous hints that Reagan would keep registration were true. On January 7, 1982, Reagan officially changed his mind. Counselor to the President Edwin Meese III read Reagan's statement at a press conference: "We live in a dangerous world. In the event of a future threat to national security, registration could save the United States as much as six weeks in mobilizing emergency manpower."

Meese called it a "practical change" based on new evidence of the value of registration in delivering persons rapidly after a mobilization, but as reporter Lee Lescaze wrote in *The Washington Post*, "There was no detailed public explanation why the new calculation had come up with so different an estimate." Recall that Reagan had previously indicated that registration would only make at best a ten-day difference.

I was incredibly angry and said so: "This decision puts the President on a collision course with a generation of draft-age men. He will need to impose the equivalent of martial law in America to track down and prosecute and imprison more than one million non-registrants." Meese also announced that there would be a grace period of between thirty and sixty days, and that late registrants would not be prosecuted during that period.

The "grace period" ended on February 28, 1982. Months passed following Attorney General William French Smith's announcement that "We will prosecute with what we have within our resources and we are prepared to enforce the law." Reagan had been given a waiver under the Privacy Act that allowed him to match up Social Security Numbers with registration rolls, but officials couldn't actually give very detailed information about non-registrants. Selective Service referred 160 non-registrants to 50 of the 94 U.S. attorneys around the country in early July. At a press conference, I called registration a "national security" fraud with regulations "riddled with constitutional and technical errors."

One afternoon in May 1982, I got a phone call from a friend who worked at a draft counseling organization. He gave me some interesting information. While riding on a city bus in Washington, he was chatting with a woman sitting next to him. She asked what he did. He explained that he was working to stop the draft registration program. She reported that she knew something about it and that she had just prepared a transcript of a high-level meeting of the Manpower Task Force on that very subject. She had a copy with her and asked if he would like a copy. When he said he would, they got off the bus and duplicated the transcript.

He was uncomfortable with what to do with this curious transcript and called me to see if I wanted to leak it to the press. I told him to drop it off and I'd see if it was a big enough deal to work with. It certainly was and I passed it on to *The Washington Post*. It was explosive and embarrassing. At the meeting were Presidential Counsellor Ed Meese, Secretary of Defense Caspar Weinberger, Assistant Secretary of the Navy for Manpower John Herrington, and the newly appointed head of Selective Service Tom Turnage. Herrington was worried that registration prosecutions would provide a rallying call for the anti-nuclear weapons movement. He urged proceeding quietly. He also made it clear that it was important to pick the right jurisdiction for your first few trials: smaller cities like Omaha. Weinberger jumped in: "Not the District of Columbia," Weinberger tried to clarify this arguably racist comment by noting that a District of Columbia prosecution would get a great deal of attention and would not be "quiet." He also said he meant that you should not begin criminal trials in a place of high unemployment. Turnage noted that there could not be "selective prosecution," however, "There is prosecutorial discretion, and I have got some names." This was followed by "joking" about who would represent the prosecutors on national television programs, including the *Phil Donohue Show.*

The transcript was front page news. I had leaked the document but at a press conference right after the comments appeared, I had to act like the whole thing surprised me. The press conference, of course, gave other news outlets the opportunity to carry the whole story the next day. This was the only time I deliberately hid knowledge of a leaked document I had unearthed. I called Herrington's comments "a stark attempt by the White House and the Pentagon to influence, in inappropriate ways, the prosecutorial policies of the Department of Justice." Neither the White House nor the Pentagon commented on the transcript, but Selective Service official Joan Lamb said it was merely a "brainstorming session," that prosecutions would occur when violators were discovered, and that the administration was not considering "selective prosecution."

I didn't believe that for one minute, telling reporters over the next few days that they would certainly prefer to prosecute white political resisters over religiously motivated ones. I also contended that they would want to avoid prosecutions of African Americans. Such prosecutions might find sympathetic juries who could be told by defense counsel that a country who didn't want to support persons of color when they were seeking educational assistance or jobs shouldn't be threatening them with jail for not signing up for registration. On this point, I was only partially correct.

The first person prosecuted was Ben Sasway of San Diego, California. He was found guilty in August and sentenced to two-and-a-half years in prison. When he was out on appeal, bail conditions applied, including not being able to leave California and a gag order prohibiting him from discussing draft resistance.

Barry Lynn joins one of the first men publicly refusing to register with Selective Service at a press conference. In spite of government threats, only 20 men were prosecuted for the felony of refusing to register. Source: Center for Conscience and War

As Sasway was being indicted, I thought it would be good to remind potential jurors in these registration cases of the doctrine of "jury nullification." This idea is that juries have an inherent right to ignore both the law and the facts if they think the underlying law is morally or otherwise wrong. No judge will explain this to jurors, but we did a modest advertising campaign in California to let potential jurors know about it through bus ads and other means. I have always liked this idea and its use in marijuana cases and efforts to prosecute doctors or women for abortions. Although *de facto* jury nullification occurred during the end of the Vietnam Era draft prosecutions, many of the new non-registrants did not even have jury trials. Other than upsetting some residents of communities where the ads appeared, our bus ads did not seem to have affected any of the few trials that did occur.

Second came Church of the Brethren resister Enten Eller, who stated his case for non-registration at a widely covered press conference. His was an unequivocal statement of religious belief from an obviously sincere man: "I am a non-registrant in order to be faithful to God, my conscience, and my church. Christ's love, the way of love, the way of concern for all peoples, the way of nonviolent peace, cannot be reconciled to involvement with the military, which uses killing and destruction, or threats of such, to achieve its ends... I have no choice but to obey the Higher Authority of God."

I was asked to speak at this press conference and noted that "the forces of history have made Enten Eller a test case. The test is whether the American legal system is capable of understanding and responding in a sensible manner to a man of unquestionable sincerity who finds himself unable to comply with a law he sees as in direct conflict with the will of God. Punishment for Enten Eller would make both a mockery of justice and a travesty of America's historic commitment to the protection of religious freedom."

Two days later, Eller appeared at a court hearing in Roanoke, Virginia, to plead "not guilty" and was released after his arraignment and the posting of a $10,000 bond in the event he didn't show up for any subsequent hearing. Judge James C. Turk sentenced him to three years' probation with 250 hours of community service and ordered him to register within 90 days. Eller again refused to register, and the U.S. Attorney asked Judge Turk to revoke probation and impose a jail sentence. Turk instead increased the amount of alternative service to two years of service to be undertaken as soon as Eller graduated from college. I attended the original sentencing but told reporters I was just there to support Eller.

The third conviction was Ohio's Mark Schmucker, a Mennonite religious resister. In an unusual comment at sentencing, Judge Ann Aldrich, who did not order him to register, concluded, "The prayers of many of us are with you." He was to spend his two years of probation working at a home for mentally impaired adults in Missouri.

Gary Eklund of Iowa was sentenced to thirty months in prison but, while on probation, got a "warning letter" that indicated he had not registered and threatening him with renewed prosecution. In a second Iowa prosecution before a different district judge, non-registrant Rusty Martin got a pretrial ruling from Judge Edward D. McManus that the government could not argue that Martin had a continuing duty to register and that it would have to prove that he willfully committed the "crime" of non-registration during the prescribed period (as in, 6 days in 1980). These cases were appealed to the Eighth Circuit; regrettably, that court upheld the idea of a "continuing duty to register."

In California, prosecutors indicted David Wayte of Pasadena. Judge Terry J. Hatter Jr. ruled that the government had engaged in highly selective prosecution by prosecuting only vocal opponents of the registration program and that this made the focus "vulnerable to the charge that those chosen for prosecution are being punished for their expression of ideas, a constitutionally protected right." The judge also ruled that the failure of the government to provide for a thirty-day comment period for President Carter's proclamation of the return to registration made the announcement invalid. The Justice Department appealed both findings. I called Hatter's decision the "death knell" for registration and alleged that "it would be irresponsible and venal for the Justice Department to indict or bring to trial resisters while this case is on its slow appeal." Unfortunately, Wayte lost the appeal at the Supreme Court in a 6-3 decision.

New England saw prosecutions of Russell Ford and Ed Hasbrouck. Hasbrouck of Boston tried to have his trial televised, arguing that the Constitution guaranteed him a truly public trial. He also filed no pretrial motions because, to Ed, the whole proceeding was more political than legal, and he wanted to expose the courts as institutions of government violence. Many years later in San Francisco, I ran into Ed, and, to this day, he has never given up trying to bring down the registration system.

Only about twenty prosecutions occurred in the early Eighties. All but one, a Laotian refugee, had actually written to Selective Service to inform them they were not registering. Then something happened. Registration rates began to tank. Moreover, the last indictment was in 1986 against an Arkansas man, Terry Kuelper. He decided to register before trial and the case was dismissed. In 1988 Gillam Kerley of Wisconsin was the last person released after a conviction, serving four months of a three-year sentence.

US News and World Report in May 2016 did a little-noticed article in which current and former Selective Service officials noted that the Justice Department had effectively given up on prosecutions of non-registrants around 1988. The Justice Department decided to rely on what Edward Frankle, former associate director of the Selective Service, called "passive enforcement," assuming that prohibitions of receiving federal funds for higher education and of getting federal employment would do the trick. In twenty-seven states, men were and are automatically registered with Selective Service when they apply for a driver's license or state-issued ID.

For a brief time, a federal court in Minnesota blocked enforcement of the so-called Solomon Amendment which barred federal financial assistance for non-registrants. However, the Supreme Court voted 6-2 in June 1984 that cutting off federal funds was constitutionally permissible. The aid cutoff was somewhat successful in increasing registration, but it is absolutely clear that there are still millions of non-registrants, and no indictments have been issued in decades.

For years, there were efforts to defund the Selective Service System, led by a former high-level staff member for Congressman Jim Weaver, Peter DeFazio, who was later himself elected to Congress. These were, unfortunately, not successful and DeFazio announced his retirement from Congress in 2021.

After working for the United Church of Christ for five years, I needed to take a break from playing a significant role in any social justice movement. While not forgetting Ramsey Clark's comment about signing on the "long haul," I wanted to cobble together a few small jobs so I could spend more time with our daughter Christina. To this day, I recall fondly taking her on picnics almost every week when she got out of pre-school.

Chapter 6

OTHER ROADS TAKEN

Our First Child

Joanne and I spent a few weeks of the summer of 1977 driving around the southwestern and northwestern United States. Our only commitment was to see Joanne's sister Mary in a summer stock production outside Seattle in Bellingham, Washington. We got to town in the middle of the afternoon and checked into our motel, eager for a swim before dinner. When we got to the pool, it was packed with people who all looked like they had come back from a war we hadn't heard had begun. They were shouting and drinking and having a much better time than it looked like we'd be having. When I asked one of the revelers what line of work he and his pals were in, he said they were the crew for *The Deer Hunter*, a film about buddies who come back to Western Pennsylvania after combat in Vietnam. The mountains in Washington State looked better than the Pennsylvania Alleghenies for Hollywood's sense of grandeur. I suggested to Joanne that we give up the swimming and return to the room. To this day, I consider Robert DeNiro and Christopher Walken to be godparents of our first child, Christina Dorcas.

Christina was not in any hurry to be born. In one effort to induce labor we went to a triple feature at an old-style drive-in theater in Southern Maryland. Alas, even sitting through *Eaten Alive* (alligators at the Starlite Motel), *Last House on the Left 2*, and *The Bad Bunch* achieved nothing to speed up the birth trajectory.

As our daughter was silently preparing to be born after a grueling labor that took twenty hours, I announced that we would have to protect her by ourselves. No government, no friends, and no family could be expected to keep her safe. I'm sure Joanne, in the midst of the pains of childbirth, had no idea what I was babbling about. I just meant that parents have a unique opportunity, and indeed a unique responsibility, for the children they choose to bring to the planet. After the birth and a day of recovery in the hospital, we drove the baby home in our yellow Toyota. It remains the most harrowing drive of my life. Never had that car appeared as fragile nor its contents as precious. This was an airbag-less tin can surrounded by bad drivers. My heart was pounding throughout the five-mile journey. However, we passed that first test of protecting our newborn. Christina was home. She was ready for the nursery, complete with a mobile, a 1970s mandated plaything that was supposed to teach concentration, lest your child become a mind-wandering, unfocused kid who would obviously be rejected for admission to Harvard.

Christina cried for weeks on end. I mean, she cried incessantly, stopping only for nursing and the occasional hour of sleep necessitated by her exhaustion. When my mother-in-law came to town, she had no magic cure, despite having raised four children. Just hold and rock. Although our daughter probably doesn't remember, her first movie with Dad was the 1957 classic, *I Was a Teenage Werewolf*, with Michael Landon. This was my effort to get her as enamored with low budget monster movies as I was. I watched it on the late-night Saturday monster movie show while rocking Christina. Joanne often commented that the crying would stop sometime before Christina went to college, she just didn't know when. The "when" turned out to be at age three months. This is a relatively common story for new parents.

Christina turned out to be a pretty easy child. She began a love of horses and, since we lived in a part of Fairfax County, Virginia, that required all lots to be five acres, there was plenty of space for a horse barn. Her love of horses may have been greater than her interest in boys, which was good for us.

She was also present in my work-life at "Bring Your Daughter to Work" days. On one occasion, she skipped school with my permission to watch me do a press conference on Project Fair Play, Americans United's effort to inform the IRS about potentially illegal political activity by religious organizations. We were also going to address our request that the Second Baptist Church in Houston be investigated immediately.

The evening before the event, Christina mentioned that her classes the next morning were political science and journalism. I pointed out that she could skip class and see my press conference instead, because there would be journalists there covering a political story. Driving to Washington the next morning after she had reviewed all the material I was going to distribute later that day, she came up with tough questions and I gave her tight, non-legalistic answers.

The questions asked at the press conference were not particularly tough. Over the next few days, Christina paid attention to the way the press covered the event and was dismayed by some of it. She was astonished at the Reverend Pat Robertson's coverage on his *700 Club* television show where he interviewed his top lawyer, Jay Sekulow. Jay said my purpose was to "muzzle" churches from discussing "major moral issues of the day." She watched the tape and issued this inquiry: "He can't really believe he is telling the truth about your project?" In this broadcast, Robertson said I was "lower than a child molester" and a "fascist." She didn't buy those characterizations either.

I think of myself as a pretty good father. However, there were two events with Christina that made me possibly less than perfect. When she went out to Berkeley, California, for college, she was without tattoos; when she came back for a winter's vacation break, she told us that she had gotten a small "sunrise" tattooed on her back. I have no problem with people getting tattoos but thought it would be clever if Joanne and I and her brother Nick would all put temporary tattoos on our backs. In those pre-9-11 times, you could meet people at their arrival gates. We did that and raised our shirts as she arrived, so she'd see the whole tattoo-ed clan. She told me she thought it was "nice," but many of the people waiting for other passengers thought it was hilarious.

Christina worked as an intern at the Democratic National Committee in one of her college summers. There were persistent rumors that President Clinton was going to visit the DNC. In this period, prior to the embarrassing revelations about White House intern Monica Lewinsky, Christina was really eager to meet him. He never actually visited. Toward the end of the summer, we had all planned to see country singer Kim Richey at the Birchmere, a club in Alexandria, Virginia, that we often visited. We had two tickets and found out that we could get a third for Christina at the door. At the last minute, she got an offer to go somewhere with friends, so she didn't join us after all. When we arrived at the venue, two large tables in the middle of the seating space had big "reserved" signs on them, something we had never seen there before. Close to the start of the show, a group of suited men and women showed up to check out the reserved space, followed shortly by President Clinton and Hillary and Vice President Gore and his wife Tipper.

After the show, as was his consistent pattern, President Clinton hung around and talked with people. The Secret Service clearly wanted him to clear out quickly, but he never did that. I always had the impression that once you said "hello," you could also tell him a story or ask his advice about a recipe, and he'd continue talking with you until dragged away. We spoke with him about some issues and then went to the car where I immediately picked up the enormous, primitive "car phone" and called Christina to ask: "Can you guess who we were just talking to?" "No." "President Clinton." She didn't believe it at first, but flaunting that we had met Bill when she had been so desperate to do so felt like a not-so-quality parenting event. She never did get to meet him.

After high school graduation, she left the next day for an internship with *The Chicago Sun Times* covering the Republican National Convention in San Diego, California. I asked my friend, columnist Clarence Page, to help her do more than bring donuts to the newspaper staff and he did that. She stayed in San Diego for a bit and then went north to the University of California, Berkeley for college, chagrined to find there was no room on campus for her.

Christina did what she has proven capable of doing for the rest of her life: making do with whatever life threw at her. With no Berkeley housing, she found a place to stay with a friend of Joanne's, a long walk from the campus. She stayed there until bringing homemade cookies to the housing staff got her an on-campus room as soon as the first few college students dropped out.

She made it through college successfully and then stayed in California where she continued the bartending she had done in Berkeley, this time working at a tiki bar in San Diego. There she learned, among other things, how to tie the stem of a maraschino cherry into a knot while holding it in her mouth. She liked the climate and met interesting people, and, with the "cherry trick" behind her, worked briefly for motivational speaker Tony Robbins, who used to have event attendees walk over hot coals. This meant a great deal of travel to exotic locations and being required to locate a gong for Robbins' presentation on some Pacific island.

Ongoing poverty in these jobs helped her decide to go to law school. Soon she was back on the East Coast at the University of Virginia Law School in Charlottesville.

During the summer months when law students were exploring internships, she tended to take up residence at our house. We'd have the chance to take her to dinner occasionally, but usually discovered she had already eaten a better lunch, paid for by the major law firms that had courted her.

She dated a number of men, several of whom I liked more than she did. She and one of them ended up with two German shepherds, one flown in from Eastern Europe who had been trained as a military "attack dog." I never got used to fearing its imminent attack on me. She ended up liking the dog more than she liked the boyfriend, but when they split up, he got both canines.

Upon graduation, she went to work at the Boston office of Wilmer-Hale. She had interned one summer at their DC office. She lived in downtown Boston and rescued a catahoula. This is a breed of dog that usually has a mottled coat (almost like a leopard) and bright blue eyes. She called him "Sinatra." When I would visit her and take him for a walk, at least once in every block, a person would ask me what he was, not necessarily seeking the name of the breed but sometimes wondering if he was some kind of exotic or supersized cat.

She left the big law firm after doing an incredible amount of work on a biotech case, only to have it settle the day before trial was to begin. This is a frequent occurrence when the risk of losing is perceived by both parties to be dangerous enough to lead to a settlement. She moved to a smaller boutique law firm and commuted by ferry across the bay from Hanover, Massachusetts.

One night at a local bar, she met Rich Omar and their relationship grew to the point that I felt an engagement was imminent. To speed that up, I suggested that the whole family meet in Hawaii over Christmas. After a few days there, Rich came up to me at a luau and told me he was planning to propose later that night, on the beach under moonlight. The next day, she had that engagement ring.

She asked me to conduct her wedding ceremony at an outdoor venue on the South Shore of Massachusetts and, of course, I agreed. It was one of the most powerful experiences of my life. When I do weddings, I always chat with some of the friends of the bride and groom and try to get them to participate with a song or a reading.

When I told people I was doing my daughter's wedding they had two questions: "How are you going to keep it together and not cry?" and "Then who is going to walk her up the aisle?" The second question was easier to answer: her brother, Nick, with whom she had been close, would walk her up the aisle.

The first was tougher. I knew so much about Christina (having known her since birth) and as I was thinking of some pleasant, but not embarrassing, incidents I might relate, I was literally sobbing in the hotel room. Should I relate how good I felt the first time she brought me a cup of soup as I was sleeping off the flu? How about the time she was watching an old Abbott and Costello movie where a gorilla comes up out of a deep hole and she went up and turned off the TV, casually mentioning that "it's scary even though I know it isn't real" (separating myth from reality at an early age). The writing was not going well since I was dealing with the whole crying thing.

I decided to have one final dad-to-unmarried daughter talk while she and the bridesmaids were having last-minute hair styling on Saturday morning. I began to cry again, prompting her to ask: "You aren't going to do that this afternoon, are you?" I didn't, but maybe there was a catch or two in my throat.

I did kick into church/state separation mode as the homily ended and I added a small twist to those semi-final words that precede that kissing part: "By the power vested in me by the Commonwealth of Massachusetts—the first state to really get this marriage thing right—I pronounce you husband and wife." Marriage equality had been legal in that state since 2004. A lot of attendees came up to me later and said they enjoyed my brief political/philosophical addition to the service.

On August 1, 2017, Christina and her husband Rich Omar gave birth (Rich was there in the delivery room) to twin daughters four weeks early. Evangelina and Victoria are, of course, the cutest children I have ever seen. Evangelina was a bit more vocal than her sister, prompting one nurse to remark: "sounds like she is ready for a picket line." They had already wrapped me and their other grandfather, David Omar, around their fingers. Three years later, brother Xavier was born.

A few days after the twins' birth, I had to officiate at the funeral of my beloved aunt Delphine Metzger in Allentown, Pennsylvania. Terrible weather had canceled most of the flights on the East Coast, so we had to rent a car to drive from Massachusetts to Allentown. Along the way I needed to pick up some decent clothes (having worn a robe for the wedding and having checked our suitcases) so we stopped at a Marshalls discount clothing store for me to pick up a sport coat and a shirt. On the way out, I noticed two sets of baby blankets and baby-safe stuffed animals: one monkey, one elephant. I took them out to the car where Joanne commented: "You know you can't buy the girls everything you think is cute, right?" Where is that rule found, I quietly wondered.

The 2+ Years of No Big Job

After my years at the UCC, it was time to rethink my career path. One part-time job was editing *The Military Law Reporter*, a bimonthly news service ironically but not surprisingly sold primarily to the Defense Department. The *Reporter* summarized case law and trends affecting service members and veterans. My predecessor was Bill Schapp, who shared my view that (this is where the irony comes in) we civilian progressive editors ought to use The *Reporter* primarily as a vehicle to help defense counsel by alerting them to useful precedents, particularly regarding procedural matters, in state and federal civilian courts that could be helpful in the military justice system. It was often said that in the military you are defense counsel only so long as you don't win cases; if you start winning you are immediately assigned to the prosecution.

During those years, I had one marvelous opportunity to see how my efforts at reform of the military discharge review system worked in real life. I was contacted by a Native American man from southern Virginia who had a very compelling story.

Weldon S. Merchant told me that he had an undesirable discharge from the Army, although he had served two tours in Vietnam and had been awarded two Purple Hearts, including one for saving a senior officer injured by friendly fire. He was given a brief period of recovery leave before returning for a third tour, and spent that time with his wife and young daughter. On the day he was to return to duty, he drove to the army base in Richmond, VA, where he was told to report. The response was, "We have no record of you even being in the military." Surprised, but not deterred, Merchant returned several times over the next few weeks and was again told that there was no record of his military status.

Eventually, he gave up. About a year later, while helping his daughter get dressed to attend Sunday School, there was a knock on his door. It was FBI agents saying he was under arrest for desertion from the Army. His explanations of his failed efforts to rejoin the military were unimpressive to them. To avoid courts-martial, he agreed to accept that undesirable discharge. The other of his Purple Hearts was from a tree falling on him when a member of his company carelessly had thrown a hand grenade. He had terrible back pain for which he could not get Veterans Administration health care. He found himself unemployable, and for a time lived in his car with his wife and daughter.

I reviewed his case and agreed to represent him at a Pentagon discharge upgrade hearing. On the day of his hearing, he came to our house for breakfast, we went over some of the details of his case. I thought he should win his upgrade, and we drove off to the Pentagon. Over lunch there, I reviewed the official documents that his panel of officers had been given to review. The summary page stated, "It is difficult to review Mr. Merchant's case because so many of his records are missing." Toward the end of the hearing, one Member said, "Mr. Lynn, so much of your case rests on the idea that Mr. Merchant's records were missing. Why should we believe you?" Diplomatically, I suggested he just read the executive summary in front of him. The hearing concluded, and on the way out, a staff member for the panel said, "There is no question that you will win."

Years later, Weldon saw me on a television show, tracked me down, and called to tell me that, with his discharge status upgraded, he finally got the V.A. care he deserved and with the pension he had earned and income from jobs, he was able to take care of his family. His obituary contains a reference to his honorable discharge.

This job was not overtly an advocacy one, but since it contained the words "military law," I found that show producers asked me to do programs on various military topics. I was with Texas Republican Senator and Senate Armed Services chair John Tower on the weekly Chamber of Commerce television show discussing military spending levels and on Ted Koppel's ABC *Nightline* discussing one of the rare Supreme Court cases involving the military and the balance between military order and discipline, and the right for officers to speak out on issues.

The writing job also gave me a chance to do something I relished: to start a small business (even though most fail within two years). I rented a second-floor office in Woodbridge, Virginia, to become part of the still nascent "home video rental" business. Most small video stores (the big chains had barely gotten into the business) dealt with both VHS and Beta cassettes. Although Beta was generally considered to provide a better picture, it did not survive the VHS competition. So, at the Video Web (with its logo of a spider watching a television caught in its web), we rented only VHS tapes. Most "mom and pop" video stores made much of their income renting pornography, usually in a small back room with a black curtain in front of it so nobody could readily see *Debbie Does Dallas, Part 8*. In spite of my later support for the First Amendment rights of people to sell adult titles, I never rented them. My store was just one large room, and I wanted the place to be family friendly.

I did have a few problems endemic to many small businesses. One employee was keeping two sets of books. When I dropped by with my lawyer one afternoon, she "found" hundreds of dollars in cash in her purse. Her firing, though, led me to hire Joanne's sister for a while, which solved the problem with her predecessor's unconventional bookkeeping. Another setback was an overnight burglary that cleaned me out of all the unrented titles in my inventory. Luckily, I had insured everything at full replacement value, so I got a chance to repurchase popular titles and get new ones.

One of my favorite customer-couples lived one county further south and had expressed on several occasions their interest in getting in the video business themselves. After I was in business for about two years and was getting weary of keeping this store open, I made the couple an offer. I would give them my entire inventory in exchange for half of the rental fees on just these tapes. They could then be able to start with a well-stocked library and could invest in things like multiple copies of brand-new releases. All I wanted was a monthly accounting of how much my old tapes had brought in. They were so scrupulously honest that my auditing only lasted two months. Then, all I did was take their check to the bank.

This business made me discover a feature of the federal income tax system that was extremely important to small corporations: depreciation. By being allowed to depreciate inventory in the year it was put into service, I could effectively erase any profit I made on the tape rentals myself or the proceeds from the couple's rentals. This video store was not "big business," but it was all I needed to see about how lucrative tax write-offs could be for depreciated property if the investments were sizable.

Chapter 7:

COMEDY AND COMEDIANS

So far, this book has largely followed the chronology of my life. However, there are some experiences, people, groups, and loves that transcend any one period in my life. I want to shift here to examining those loves of my life because all of my life I have survived the demands of my job by immersing myself in comedy, music, and movies.

As I mentioned earlier, my father always added some humor in the notes he wrote for his Cat & Dog stock-trading club. He was also eager to take me to see the classic comedies he had watched as a teenager, which were, sadly, hard to find in the pre-streaming, pre-cable, pre-VHS tapes era. I remember spending an evening with my parents in our Bethlehem recreation room laughing nearly to the exclusion of breathing at a stand-up set by Buddy Hackett on the *Tonight Show* with Johnny Carson about being lonely. My dad's love of humor was so contagious that it has followed me all through my life. I also came to realize that many comedians had a social conscience.

Paul Krassner

I hoped my parents didn't see one particular magazine when it arrived during my senior year in high school. No, it wasn't *Playboy*—though I think my father had a few of those hidden around. It was a magazine done on newsprint called *The Realist*, edited by Paul Krassner. It was very controversial because it was so far left and made its points in such brilliant ways. For example, Paul and one of his women friends, dubbed "the Realist Nun," would do outrageous things in public while she was dressed in full habit.

After the Kennedy assassination and the book on the subject by William Manchester, Paul did a piece called "The Parts That Were Left Out of the Manchester Book." He claimed, among other things, that Lyndon Johnson had sex with Kennedy's corpse on the plane from Dallas to Washington. Another particularly provocative piece was a cartoon centerfold called "The Disneyland Orgy" that displayed all those cute Disney cartoon characters engaged in a multitude of sexual activities.

Paul was once on rabid right winger Joe Pyne's television show, and Pyne asked him why he still had acne. Paul's response was, "Since we are discussing personal matters do you take off your wooden leg [which Pyne had] when you have sex." Paul wouldn't put up with crap from anyone.

One of the best things about this magazine was that it mixed satire and actual stories so well that people sometimes couldn't tell the difference. Even before I met Paul in person for the first time, a college friend, Sandy Weinberg, and I created a Sunday evening radio show broadcast from campus to a two-block radius of the campus. It was called *The Kroyt Report*. The name came from the first record album we picked up before our first broadcast—a classical record from the Kroit Quartet (we accidentally misspelled their name). The purpose of the show was to mix actual stories from the United Press International wire that sounded like they couldn't possibly be true with stories we made up that sounded like they might be true but weren't. The purpose was to highlight to listeners that you can't always believe what you hear in the media. Now, you could call it a prescient warning about "fake news."

Our show was reasonably successful until its final edition before graduation. At the suggestion of singer John Denver (to whom I fed a tuna fish sandwich in my apartment after a show), we had driven all Friday night with Joanne and a high school friend of Joanne's, then at Virginia's William and Mary College, and her blind date, a Dickinson student named Tom James, to Virginia Beach to see a total eclipse of the sun on Saturday. It was a powerful sight as the shadow of the sun swept out into the ocean. But we discovered, in this pre-credit card era, as we ate some breakfast, that we didn't have enough money to get home (and I had to buy that sweatshirt depicting the eclipse with a few dollars we had scraped together). When we got to William and Mary College to drop off Joanne's friend, she gave us ten dollars to buy gas and a dessert at Howard Johnson's. This trek was exhausting, and I slept most of Sunday and then realized I did not have the energy to plow through days of UPI tickers. My solution: let's do a show about me committing suicide.

Sandy went out and interviewed students about this catastrophe. One said: "This is terrible because he owed me five dollars"; another "I never really liked that guy." Even Joanne was taped, noting her "disappointment" with my passing. This was absolutely tasteless, more so because Sandy and I also put up a makeshift "shrine" outside the cafeteria, complete with a rock with my birth and death dates scrawled on it with chalk and some drooping flowers. We were fired by the station. Who could blame them?

I ran the Cultural Affairs series at Dickinson College after wresting it away from control by a faculty member who generally booked opera singers and pianists of little interest to students and only a tad more interest to the retirees in the Carlisle community. He did have the good sense to hire a few popular culture giants of the late Sixties, including the Canadian folk duo of Ian and Sylvia and the incredible Nina Simone. However, I created a student committee that booked folksingers like Denver, Doc Watson and Tom Rush, the traveling troupe of *Hair* (nudity included), poet LeRoi Jones (who later changed his name to Amiri Baraka), and other icons of interest to African American students and women. During our senior year, Judy Collins cancelled two dates during her time of great success with Joni Mitchell's "Both Sides Now" and her tempestuous dealings with drugs. We had a few dollars left so I recommended that we have Paul Krassner come to campus.

Paul came and did a terrific, funny speech to the students and faculty. We hung around a bit after the show, and I was scheduled to take him to the airport the next morning. As I dropped him at his hotel, I asked him if he needed a wake-up call. "No," he said, "I don't even use an alarm clock. I just wake up when I'm supposed to." He was there to go to the airport as planned.

In May 1970, horrific shootings of students at Jackson State and Kent State caused campuses to erupt with righteous anger at the Nixon Administration and all the warmongering. At Kent State, the shooters were members of the Ohio National Guard, ironically one of the safest military assignments during the Vietnam War. At Dickinson, much of the outrage was directed at Carlisle's Army War College, a training ground for Defense Department personnel, rumored to be a place where people learned brutal interrogation techniques and propaganda writing. I proposed to a student body meeting late on the night after Kent State to march to the War College, saying: "The time for talk is over. ... [T]his is the brain trust of the war machine. We need to march there and try to close it down." Students were wildly enthusiastic about this not particularly well-conceived idea, which was finally nixed when Dickinson's President, Howard Rubendall, warned the student body that there were reports of armed citizens waiting for any marchers. Students heeded his warning and voted to march a few days later.

I was tasked with finding a speaker for the protest and getting a bus company to take a large number of students to Washington for the big march on Saturday. Contacting Paul Krassner was the easier part and he eagerly agreed to come. Most bus companies in central Pennsylvania wouldn't even consider hiring out eight or nine buses for such a radical endeavor. Surprisingly, the company that ran Gettysburg Battlefield Tours was willing to do so. So, growing from eight people who had gone to New York City for an anti-war demonstration in 1966, we moved eight busloads that day to Washington, DC. In addition, many other folks drove themselves. Protestors loved taking photographs of a bunch of their colleagues arriving in buses emblazoned with the words "Gettysburg Battlefield Tours."

Although I continued to subscribe to *The Realist*, I lost track of Paul for a number of decades. He was on a short-lived Fox network (before the Fox News Network) television show called *The Wilton North Report*, but his humor might have been just a bit too raw for television as he told stories on Friday nights and introduced underground videos for the hosts Phil Cowen and Paul Robins. I used to watch the show on Friday nights and saw that it had incredibly weird ideas about what to cover. In one bizarre incident, the show did a piece on a basketball team in South Carolina that had not had a win in five years but pulled off a victory the one night the camera crew was there. In what may have been one of the understatements of the decade, the President of the network explained the cancellation of *The Wilton North Report;* he said the show was "a bit too ambitious."

Paul was a close friend of songwriter Phil Ochs. It was said of Phil by his sister Sonny: "Phil would hold a fundraiser for someone who needed a new pair of shoes." Paul would have a fundraiser for someone who needed a new pair of socks.

Regrettably, Paul was not very well known. He often said to me: "If I had gotten arrested in Chicago in 1968, I would have been as famous as Bobby Seale and Abbie Hoffman." Although said jokingly, even his masterful creation of the "Yippie" movement didn't get the credit it deserved.

While fundraising later for Americans United for Separation of Church and State, I ran into a number of our largest donors who shared their love of Paul and *The Realist.* Paul and I started up an email relationship again and he joined me on my *Cultureshocks* radio program a few times. He was not in good health, but he volunteered to do a fundraiser for us. Like many who don't have enough disposable income to get their teeth fixed, Paul had dental problems that were flaring up as we were trying to put that fundraising event together. "Dinner with Paul" was supposed to happen in Utah, but, sadly, it did not.

When he was a guest on my podcast *Cultureshocks* in 2019, Paul was strangely reticent and never mentioned how ill he was. He died in July 2019. I loved Paul and was honored when he asked me to do a blurb for his latest book. That book was never published.

Lewis Black

Las Vegas is a fun city to visit, even if your idea of gambling is buying a lottery ticket only when the jackpot is over $100 million dollars. I used to get invited to speak at conventions held in that city and loved it so long as I didn't have to be there more than two nights, one night to see a magician and the other to see a comedian. One time I had to be there for three nights and ended up renting a car and driving forty miles into the desert to watch the stars.

I saw some great magic—David Copperfield, the Mentalist, and others—and a mixed bag of comics. The Improv is always a good show. Most people show up as a last-minute thing, but I meticulously planned to go and bought my ticket well in advance. Buying a ticket that way meant I invariably got a front seat at a table next to the stage. I was usually there by myself for the whole show. This opened me up to insults and questions from the comedians, which was just fine by me. One woman comedian asked me if I knew what kind of show this was, since I was sitting up close. She assured me she would not be taking off her clothes.

Occasionally, the comedian was an established "name" like Andrew Dice Clay (not exactly my cup of tea) and Lewis Black. I had seen Lewis on television and shelled out over $100 for a space without a seat at one of the casinos. He was absolutely brilliant—well worth the ticket price.

Fast forward to 2013. I was on vacation with Joanne in Japan when I got a call from my office. Duane Davis, the jack of all trades there, said he wanted to pass on information he thought I'd like. I had just been offered the Puffin Foundation award for "creative citizenship." He said someone had called him from the Foundation and he jokingly said he'd pass on any message, particularly if the award "came with a million dollars." She said, "No, but it does have $100,000 attached." When I looked this up on the internet before going on a day of cave exploring, I realized this was a very big deal. Some of my greatest heroes and sheroes had received it in past years: Tony Kushner of *Angels in America* fame and Planned Parenthood President Cecile Richards. The money came with no strings attached. After thinking for about two minutes that I could buy a Lexus with it, I knew I would just return it to Americans United. This foundation clearly was impressed with our work, and, since it also made grants to young musicians, they were particularly happy to hear about the Americans United project, Voices United for Separation of Church and State.

When I got home and got more details, I learned that Lewis Black was going to be the emcee the night of the awards ceremony in New York City. This was a wonderful add-on.

The award required me to make a fifteen-minute acceptance speech, but I like writing speeches. I also have never given a speech without interjecting some humor. Since the awards were given in mid-December, I wrote a few jokes about the nonsensical "war on Christmas" idea being pushed by rightwing pundits like Bill O'Reilly and Sean Hannity. During Lewis' introduction to the whole event, he told a few jokes about the same subject, so over the salad, I had to come up with some new material. After all, this guy was my favorite living comedian, and I couldn't possibly compete with him.

Cecile Richards introduced me, telling the audience that I had once told her that when anti-evolutionists were asked how Noah fit dinosaurs into the Ark, they usually said, "they were baby dinosaurs." I got up, thanked the family that financed the award, and noted, "I would also like to thank you for having Lewis Black as emcee because this is the first time I didn't have to shell out $125 to hear him." As I was saying it, I looked at him in part out of fear that he wouldn't like the comment, but he seemed to be enjoying it. I went on with the speech, and made some funny comments about Hobby Lobby, which was in litigation at the time, claiming to have a protected "religious belief" against providing contraceptives to women employees, a requirement of the Affordable Care Act. I think I said, "When one of the do-it-yourself pink flamingos they sell starts singing 'Nearer My God to Thee,' maybe I will believe they have some corporate religious belief." I included a few other gems like that.

Lewis came up after the dinner was over and said, "Maybe you could open for me sometime." I thought that was nice, but I took it as the same kind of thing broadcaster Larry King once said to me and my radio partner Pat Korten one night after his television show on CNN: "You guys are going to be the next big thing in radio." Very nice but we were both fired a few weeks later. Lewis did give me his private email and we occasionally corresponded for the next few years.

I followed up with Lewis when he said he'd like to do something for Americans United's Voices United series. We arranged for a show in

September 2014 featuring him, Lizz Winstead, and Kate Clinton at the 92nd Street Y, a popular venue in New York City. As people were coming in, I had to open the program with a few serious comments about the work of Americans United and some of the recent bad decisions of the Supreme Court. This being a comedy night, I couldn't suppress my inner amateur comic. When I came onstage, I asked, "Wouldn't you be surprised if this wasn't a politics and comedy night, but we just got you here to preview Apple's launch of the iPhone 6?" Then I launched into some of the weird stuff denizens of the Religious Right had said or done just over the past forty-eight hours. I didn't have to joke about it; I just had to say what they did to get audience laughs.

Once at a humanist conference in Arizona, comedian Julia Sweeny (who played the gender-non-specific "Pat" on Saturday Night Live for several seasons) came up to me after a speech and said she appreciated that I got laughs throughout the presentation. I thanked her, even though most of those laughs came from merely repeating quotes from right wingers.

This event happened just days after the death of Joan Rivers and the suicide of Robin Williams. In a conversation between Lewis and Lizz, they discussed their own recollections of both of them. Lewis had written a scathing response to Rush Limbaugh's offensive claim linking Williams' suicide to his liberalism. Lizz had tweeted about how Rivers had opened up possibilities for women comedians that were unparalleled when Rivers started in clubs and on late night television. This was very moving.

After a break, it was time for me to ask all three some questions about comedy and politics. We explored whether you can be a politically conservative comedian, or do they just try to pass off mean-spirited attack rhetoric as comedy. I thought the latter, and the Fox News' late night "comedy" show with Greg Gutfeld in 2020 proved my point. Another question we explored was whether a comedian like Tina Fey playing Sarah Palin on *Saturday Night Live* really damaged Palin's credibility. Or do politicians just do that to themselves? Lizz pointed out that a lot of what Tina Fey did was simply reciting actual comments Palin had made. We also opined about whether cracks about tragic events were ever appropriate.

I had once heard the author of *Catch 22*, Joseph Heller, answer a questioner who asked him whether that book had helped spur opposition to the war in Vietnam. "Novels don't have that power. If we had depended on *Uncle Tom's Cabin* to end slavery, little Eliza would still be crossing the ice." Lewis said that he was "not going to bring the government to its knees by telling a joke. I'm not storming the Bastille." I'm not sure I agree because to mock the affectations of power by government officials can give listeners a sense of her or his individual capacity as advocate or voter to make up their own mind. Moreover, wit can sometimes force people on the right (and occasionally on the left as well) to confront hypocritical positions.

Lewis invited me to see his presentation at the National Press Club several years later. He had also invited a conservative activist he knew from DC. It was a wonderful lunch, and I had a chance to meet Black's extraordinary parents, both in their upper nineties at the time, whom he'd occasionally mention in his shows. The last time somebody had invited me to a presentation at the Press Club was to see the President of the Church of Scientology. Angela Cartwright, the voice of Lisa Simpson, was a Scientologist at the time and was at our table. She autographed a bookmark for my son who, like the rest of the family, always watched *The Simpsons*.

Joanne and I discovered that one of the charities that Lewis supported was "Children of the Forest," a program to provide funds for a group of children in Southeast Asia to attend institutions of higher learning. It sounded like a great program, and we started contributing $1,000 a year to it, which it turned out, guaranteed us a "meet and great" opportunity with Lewis. I know that I could have just asked to see him, but I am extremely uncomfortable asking any performers for special favors. My philosophy is that, if I like the artist and the venue, I should contribute to both by buying my tickets, not asking for them for free. We always had a wonderful time chatting with him.

In 2018, I decided to retire after 25 years from my position leading Americans United for Separation of Church and State. The Board wanted to have a "going away" event for me. Writing to Lewis to consider hosting felt like a long shot, but he enthusiastically said he'd be happy to do it. I bumped into Lewis the night before my retirement gala as we were both checking into a hotel, and he asked if I wanted to join him at a seafood restaurant to watch the last game of the World Series. As we were walking to the restaurant about ten blocks away, one of his legions of fans asked him if he could take a selfie with the two of them. When Lewis said "sure," he waited almost three-minutes for the fellow to figure out how to take a selfie and it didn't bother Lewis at all. At the restaurant he chatted with many of the servers whom he remembered from previous visits.

Just three weeks after this retirement event, Joanne and I were visiting her ninety-year-old mother in Indiana, Pennsylvania. On the day after Thanksgiving, after a brief breakfast buffet at the motel we were staying in, I went back to the room, laid down, and couldn't get up to brush my teeth. I was exhausted and just wanted to go home. When I mentioned to Joanne that my left arm didn't seem right, she said we wouldn't be going home; we'd be going to the local emergency room. After briefly protesting that idea, I recalled the many times she had proven to be smarter than I was and went to the hospital. The emergency room physician knew I was having a serious heart problem, but it had no cardiac surgery unit. After transfer to the Cleveland Clinic three days later, and a total of three hospital stays, I went home. During one of those stays, a thirty-six-hour anesthesia, my right vocal cord was paralyzed and for months I could not speak above a whisper. I chronicled all this in brief cellphone photos—annotated with ironic comments—and people knew that bad things were happening.

I gradually started to go out to hear music and see movies. I was also scheduled to see Lewis at the Warner Theater in Washington. He wrote me a note that asked me to perform a "rant" after his set, even if I had to whisper it. This was a great opportunity, but it was frightening. I had not been scared of public speaking since junior high school, but this had all the possibilities of a fiasco, since I was still really weak, my vocal cords were unreliable, and this rant wouldn't happen until 10:00 p.m.

When I got to the Warner and went backstage, one of Lewis' managers asked him, "Which one of your rants is Barry going to read?" and Lewis accurately noted, "I'm pretty sure he has written his own." I had spent days writing it and it went over well enough that I said at the end, "Thanks for listening and not making this feel like an episode of the Showtime series *I'm Dying Up Here*." That night I felt that my groove was coming back enough, if a little less deep than usual.

I still see Lewis every six months or so. He is a very generous man.

John Fuegelsang

I've met no better radio interviewer than John Fuegelsang, whose show *Tell Me Everything* airs on XM/Sirius, the satellite radio operation. We had occasionally been guests of Ed Schultz on Fridays, usually to discuss some Religious Right activity that had occurred that week or was scheduled for the weekend. Although I had seen the film *Coyote Ugly*, I had somehow not noticed that John was in it, possibly distracted by Piper Perabo who was also in the movie. John had also been on the Bill Maher show with Jerry Falwell, but I had quit watching Maher long before. John had a tremendous knowledge of the Bible, and, when I chatted with him the first time I was on his radio show, he said he was born to a brother and sister, not some incestuous relationship but the marriage of a Franciscan brother and a nun who had worked with lepers for a decade or so of her life. They had met and fallen in love. Both left their religious orders without abandoning Catholicism. John is thus well-versed in Christian beliefs and easily combats Religious Right callers and tweeters who challenge his arguments, which include his accurate claims that Donald Trump has never taken a position in line with the teachings of Jesus.

I started going on John's radio show in New York to discuss core church-state issues during the last year or so of my work at Americans United. I was given only thirty minutes because John's talented producer at the time, Neal Golub, with John had decided that thirty minutes was the max to hold listener attention. I was often in New York to raise money for Americans United and it was always good to say to a potential donor over lunch: "Thanks for lunch and I'm on my way to do a satellite radio show." I probably got a few subscribers to XM/Sirius in the process.

As I was nearing retirement, John said after one show that he was trying to mix activists and academics in panels with professional comedians and kick around issues in the news: "Would you be interested in that?" I said "Of course" and then asked him if he'd like to do a brief interview for a video at my retirement event. He agreed and called me a "bodhisattva" in the clip. For about two months I had a chance to be on panels with a number of clever New York comedians, including Krystal Kamenides, Leah Bonnema, Mark Anthony Ramirez, Liz Miele, Keith Price, and Rhonda Hansome. When I chatted with them after the shows, I realized that, even as it was tough making a living as a travelling musician, it was much harder to do it as a comic. I learned that some clubs would only book you if you could guarantee that you could get twenty paying friends to the show.

Right before my retirement, John said: "Now that you will be retired, you can do the show more often." This was very encouraging, but I wouldn't have the excuse of raising money in New York and thought it would be too expensive to come up even once a month on the train or bus. Then, just weeks after my retirement gala, the health calamity hit, putting me in three hospitals over three months.

As I recovered over a few months, I thought it would be fun to go be on John's show again, so I arranged it with his new producer, Xorje Olivares. When I got to the lobby of the XM/Sirius office suites, I ran into David Feldman. I knew he had won several Emmys for comedy writing, and I had been on John's show panels with him a few times. He said that he had heard I had some pretty serious medical issues and inquired about "what I was going to talk about." My response was quick: "Anything but being sick." David said "No, that is the only thing you talk about." So, I did and the other comics on the panel chimed in with their jokes.

At one point I mentioned that my carotid artery and my aortic valve had been replaced with cow tissue and "the only thing that really pisses me off about that is that I am still unable to give milk." Perhaps it was the lameness of that joke, but callers to the show began making similarly marginal cow jokes—e.g., don't you like "moovies"?— for most of the rest of the hour.

This show really made me feel that I could make a comeback to normalcy even if I couldn't sound like I used to. So, I was perpetually thankful for David's insistence on what to talk about.

Obsessing over what my voice sounded like became a major concern of my life at that time. I can still get rattled when I make phone calls because I don't think I sound "normal," but people keep assuring me that I sound "just like you used to." In 2021, a visit to my ENT (Ear-Nose-Throat) doctor, after passing a small camera through my nasal passage, confirmed that the vocal cord was moving normally again.

Feldman and I have become close friends. After straightening him out on some issues—like why churches shouldn't be able to endorse political candidates but should speak to moral issues and why the military draft will not prevent future wars—I was invited to do his podcast every week. His show is quite extraordinary. He airs two each week, Tuesday and Friday, and they are often six or seven hours long. In addition, during the COVID-19 crisis he began holding "office hours" the first weekend of each month where some of his guests can interact on Zoom with his listeners. It starts at 9 p.m. on Friday and is often still going at 10 p.m. on Saturday. When I joined "office hours," my original function was to do an "invocation" and answer questions from the audience. I usually disengage at about 11:30 p.m. It is a fascinating collection of people who can speak about Latin American history; Chinese economic policy; and rock music—sometimes out of the same mouth. He jokes that it is a "cult," which may not be far from the truth. I prefer to think of us regulars as a smarter and more articulate version of Howard Stern's *Whack Pack*.

Joanne joined us in April of 2020 to give us her read on COVID. At this time many physician pontificators in the media were minimizing the threat. She explained that we would probably have 500,000 deaths in the United States alone. She backed it up, answered questions from the inquiries in the "chat room" of the Zoom meeting, and did not sugarcoat the dangers. All she said turned out to be true. In the "chat room" I noticed comments like: "How did Barry hook up with someone this smart?" I could only answer: "It's a mystery to me."

My Own Forays into Stand-up Comedy

My first public stand-up act was at a Planned Parenthood comedy fundraiser in Washington at the Improv, where actual comedians were interspersed with activists for an evening of fun. I had never done stand-up, except in the context of serious talks, but the guy who recruited me, Tim Howe, said that wasn't a problem because one of professionals would be matched with each amateur to help us get a few minutes of material prepared.

A week before the event, Howe called to say that "the professionals just didn't have the time to work with the amateurs." Since I believed I had already developed some possibly good material, I told him that wouldn't be a problem. In fact, this news dramatically increased my anxiety. One day before the event, he called again and sheepishly announced that "all of the other amateurs had dropped out." I told him I was disappointed, but would still do the show. My anxiety soared.

The night of the show, Joanne was out of town, but our daughter was in DC working as a summer clerk for a major law firm and was eager to come. The first professional was announced as Mimi Gonzalez "New York City's best known Hispanic Bisexual Comedian." She was terrific and told a lot of anti-religion and pro-sex jokes. I was up next and the guy who recruited me said "I have never known you to be nervous, but you don't look too good," the kind of discomfiting words I didn't need to hear. Walking up the narrow, dark corridor to the stage, I was as uncomfortable as I ever recalled being in the past fifty years.

The M.C. for the night, Bob Somerby, whose college roommates had been Al Gore and Tommy Lee Jones, did my introduction, calling me "every progressive's favorite preacher because he gets to yell at Ann Coulter." Then he mentioned Americans United for Separation of Church and State, which launched the audience into thunderous applause. I immediately thought about quitting while I was ahead but soldiered on.

As I started, I noted that Ms. Gonzalez was looking at the stage. I said: "I just wanted to say that I was not offended by the anti-religion jokes, but that I had a complaint about one of the sex jokes—that the only bad thing about porn is that it teaches men that the only way to have sex is in rhythm with bad rock songs." I noted, "I know that you can make love to Peter, Paul and Mary records and I have two planned children to prove it, and one is right here in the audience." Christina stood up, and people really laughed. The rest of my set went well, with the exception of a joke about a snail I stole from a live recording of a Chicago folksinger, Michael Smith. I still think it is funny. Here it is: A snail was mugged by two turtles. When the police arrived and asked what happened, the snail replied, "I don't know. It happened so fast."

A father actively involved with Parents and Friends of Lesbians and Gays (PFLAG) asked if I would go to Utah where the local school system was having some trouble because a Gay-Straight Student Alliance club wanted to meet in the high school but had been denied the right to do so. I called and asked whether he wanted me to be funny or inspirational. He answered, "both." PFLAG had hired a "house band." At the run through, I asked if they could play "Stairway to Heaven" when I got on stage, and we decided I would do some funny stories at a standup mike and the more serious stuff from a podium center right.

The other folks at this program were terrific: including well-known comic Kate Clinton and the extraordinary couple Phyllis Lyons and Del Martin, the first two women who obtained a marriage license (later revoked by a court) in 2004 in California. After it was over, Catie Curtis came over and told me how much she appreciated what I had said, and Kate said: "It is so rare to hear political comedy these days." Those were the pre-Trump days, obviously. At the reception afterward, one young lesbian brought her girlfriend over to where I was standing and said, "He's so adorable." That was nice. When I mentioned this incident at a staff meeting a few days later, Beth Corbin, our national field director (herself a lesbian), said: "You should just put on your resume that young lesbians find you adorable."

Catie and I took a cab to the airport early the next morning and I told her just how great her music was and how I owned every record of hers ever made. Joanne and I saw her a few times at clubs around Washington and chatted about how her life and career were going. Catie would soon become an even more substantial player in my life at AU.

159

Barry Lynn, Tom Paxton, and the Don Juans.

Chapter 8

AMERICANA MUSIC

Music is quite a force for social change. Certainly, music has been quite an influence on me and an important component of achieving social justice.

I had been fascinated with the relationship between art and politics since I was in high school. One Sunday night in 1966, I was listening to the big Magnavox radio in our living room and tuned in to a barely audible station in Philadelphia where Gene Shay was playing something called folk music. He had just set up a song by a person who was singing about all the ways you could get out of the military draft, like telling the draft board: "I'm only eighteen, I got a ruptured spleen, and I always carry a purse...When the bombshell hits, I get epileptic fits and I'm addicted to a thousand drugs." You get the picture. Some people may recognize them as lyrics to Phil Ochs' "Draft Dodger Rag." Ochs made a powerful statement: if enough people made these crazy excuses, the country could not have the "glorious" war they wanted.

Finding the album *I Ain't Marching Anymore* took me months. I finally located it in Speedy's, an Allentown, Pennsylvania, record store. One spin and I was hooked. People were using their music to make political statements and were apparently even making money saying things I didn't know you could promote in public. Art, music, and film can sometimes bypass rational argument and intellectual analysis and have a tremendous impact. You can feel it first and figure it out later. And Ochs' lyrics were blunt and potent. They were a lot more direct than trying to figure out what lessons were contained in songs about flowering lemon trees or how many skies a white dove was sailing in.

My first foray into booking musical acts was as head of Dickinson College's Cultural Affairs series. I felt that, since I never had a musically talented nerve in my body, I could at least enjoy the glow around people who could make music. To this day, I cannot truly understand what jazz "is," but with singer-songwriters, their passions and missions are right out front and readily accessible.

When we first moved to Boston, I made some overtures to acoustic music management companies. They weren't looking for part-time help, so this never panned out.

Joanne and some other first-year medical students had been doing some testing of lead in apartments around Boston and had found startling concentrations of this poisonous paint in many places, including our Boston University graduate student housing. I thought we might raise money for the cause. Boston had just opened a civic auditorium, the John B. Hynes Center. I found a music promoter in Rhode Island named "Skip" Chernov and convinced him to help me put together a musical event to raise funds for lead eradication. Skip said that, if I could get the city to open the venue, he would get the talent to perform. The management at Hynes agreed to give us the venue virtually cost-free. Chernov got Grand Funk Railroad, Melanie, local favorite Chris Smither, and Jonathan Edwards. When a story about this appeared in the *Boston Phoenix*, an important local music and politics weekly, the Hynes manager called me to tell me that Hynes had cancelled the event because "We don't want to open the place with rock n roll."

Only many years later, with Voices United, did I get to return to arranging events and booking acts.

Music Makes the Message Clearer—Voices United

Many people never buy a recording of a musician unless they have seen that person live and in person. That is, unless they can't afford the ticket price to go to a concert. I am not one of those people. I have always purchased lots of music from people whom I have only heard on the radio or read about in the music publications I respect.

Singer-songwriter and "folk rock goddess" (according to *The New Yorker*) Catie Curtis is definitely in that category. Thus, I had been delighted to learn that she and I would both be on that program at the national convention of PFLAG in Salt Lake City, Utah, in 1995.

Later, she agreed to sing in a two-hour video program Americans United did with a sister organization called The Interfaith Alliance. That show was produced by Adam Klugman, Jack's son and a popular radio host in California, and featured Kevin Bacon and his brother's band, actor/comedian Marc Maron, and a host of AU clients who fought against creationism, religious indoctrination in the military, laws against Wiccan religious practice, and efforts to stop abortion services in rural America. The whole thing was emceed by actor Peter Coyote, also the voice of so many world-class documentaries. Catie was joined that night by John Jennings, who was Mary Chapin Carpenter's lead guitarist and a fine singer in his own right. The two-hour show was edited overnight and then aired in movie theaters around the country the next day.

I kept in touch with Catie and John, and John and I had a pre-Thanksgiving lunch. We had those sandwiches that mix turkey, filling, cranberry sauce, and gravy. I asked him if he thought we could do a fundraising concert in DC like other progressive non-profits had done recently. He said: "We could, but let's think bigger." How much bigger? "How about doing a concert in every state on the same weekend next fall?" It was a breathtaking idea and I left feeling excited by the prospect but petrified about how such a venture could be put together and who could organize it. Mary Chapin Carpenter did an interview once where she mentioned that she and John used to hang around in his basement music studio and "diddled around" with music, "That's the way John is. John is like 'Let's do it.' He doesn't see hurdles. I see hurdles." Nothing summed up my relationship with John any better.

John Jennings and I spent a few days at the International Folk Alliance conference in Memphis that spring, doing some recruiting.

All kinds of songwriters, producers, and managers loved the idea and volunteered to try to be a part of it. Dave Marsh, the well-known music critic for *Rolling Stone*, with whom I had worked during the rock and rap censorship wars some years earlier, saw me in the audience of his workshop on "music and politics" and asked me to say a few words. Singers gave me their CDs or told me something in their lives that connected them to the separationist cause. I stayed up until 3 a.m. for three days and was sure we had a good chance of having a music event in every state pushing separation of church and state.

Catie and I had a phone call a few days later and I told her about John's idea but my concern about who could put this together. Tentatively she advanced the idea, "Maybe I could do this." I had not expected that response and had just thought maybe she knew of some company that did such things. Of course, she was the person to do it—she had a sterling reputation from fellow musicians for her grit and integrity. We worked out a way to put her on the Americans United payroll. That's where the fun began.

We ended up doing three years of *Voices United for Separation of Church and State* with hundreds of artists participating—from singers like Ani DiFranco, Dar Williams and Dan Bern to comedians like Lizz Winstead, Sarah Silverman and Russell Brand. Planning costs for much of the second and third years were financed by that Puffin Award. What was so fascinating was that almost no one was neutral or negative; everyone worked hard to support the cause. A close friend of Bruce Springsteen told me that Bruce was impressed with the scope of this endeavor.

The first season of *Voices United for Separation of Church and State* got a show or two in every state and it was a wild and eclectic event. A total of seventy-four shows in fifty states (and DC) spread the message and recruited new people. My daughter Christina lived in Massachusetts and went to a show in Newton and started chatting with a man sitting next to her. He turned out to be Ellery Schempp, the plaintiff in the famous 1963 Supreme Court case *Abington School District v. Schempp* which ended prayers and Bible reading in public schools. Morris Dees, one of the founders of the Southern Poverty Law Center, hosted blues singer and activist Guy Davis (son of civil rights icons Ossie Davis and Ruby Dee). When the original venue for a Mississippi show got cold feet, a Jackson restaurant called the "Julip Restaurant" jumped in to offer the place, and a wonderful singer from Maine, Jenna Lindbo, flew in to do a show which she described afterward as "full of energy." In New Orleans, a great show happened in Ward 8, which had been heavily damaged by Hurricane Katrina, headlined by poet Chuck Perkins and a group of accompanying musicians for slam poetry with a strong focus on racial justice.

The culmination of that first season was a show in Los Angeles at the El Ray Theater. It had a great lineup: Catie Curtis, songwriter Mary Gauthier, Sarah Silverman (whose sister is a rabbi who used to rent Catie's house near Boston for a few weeks each summer), and Russell Brand. There is a great deal of wealth in Los Angeles, and we expected a good turnout. I often call the box office to get an idea of how ticket sales were going for any show I produce. When I called the El Rey about a week before the show I was told "There are only $1000 'meet and greet' tickets available." For me, this was fabulous news because it meant that all of the other tickets, down to the $50 ones, were gone—and the income to Americans United would be substantial.

Unfortunately, something had gone horribly wrong. When a few of us showed up several hours before the show, the place was a dead zone. The woman at the box office said, "Oh, there are plenty of tickets available." When I explained that I was the guy putting on the event she told me that only 52 tickets had been sold (out of over 500). I immediately put calls into some of our members that I was certain would be there and was told they weren't coming "because the only tickets cost $1,000 and that is too rich for my blood."

The whole thing was humiliating. Everyone was completely professional about it but clearly unhappy as well. Sarah told me how popular she was in the area and was convinced (as was Mary) that the event had been "sabotaged." There was no way to even begin to explore that and whenever I saw Sarah or Mary after that they still bring it up as an unexplained phenomenon. To this day both of them believe there was a deliberate effort to make ticket sales decline.

I learned a great deal about asking artists to "gift" a night to the cause. We shouldn't expect a musician to give up a gig in a major city gratis, so we often made deals for a dramatically reduced fee, then found other performers who wanted the opportunity to perform with that "big name" artist. I do like "win/win" situations and found plenty of them. Joanne and I put on a number of "house concerts" and would "upsell" tickets so that people who were willing and able to donate $250 got a front row seat, some homemade lasagna, and a chance to dialogue with the artists. We learned from Dar Williams about the catastrophic decline of butterflies while John Gorka revealed the occasional rigors of the life of a traveling artist.

There were a lot of highlights to these events, but two of them stand out to this day. Sarah Silverman was part of a number of these shows, and she always brought fabulous comics with her. In 2013, at the Largo at the Coronet, for example, she had Natasha Leggero, Tig Notaro, and Rob Delaney with her. Natasha came out first, admitted she didn't know much about Americans United and asked for a volunteer to come up and discuss why separation of church and state was so important. She chose me, sitting in the front row. I had assumed this had been set up by Sarah Stevenson, our major gifts officer, who was with me that night, but she swears it was not. As I was walking up to the stage, I said: "You came to the right place. I'm the guy who runs Americans United." During the interview, she said it was nice to have someone to interview who didn't have alcohol on his breath. I asked her about her interviewing skills, after pointing out that "I have been interviewed by the best: Phil Donahue, William F. Buckley, Jr. and even, not the best: Laura Ingraham and Bill O'Reilly." She asserted that her skills were fine and then managed to work some of the more serious examples of bad church/state actors into the rest of her set.

Sarah Silverman had also arranged one night for the terrific comic Jen Kirkman to show up and asked me to introduce her. I knew nothing about her, but Sarah said, "Just say her name and her fans will applaud." I told just one story before the introduction about a recent trip I had taken in one of the most conservative parts of Maryland. "I was recently on a kayaking trip on a river in Southern Maryland and noticed a large Confederate flag on someone's lawn near the water. I wasn't surprised to see it, given the voting pattern in that part of the state, but couldn't figure out what the shape was in the middle of the stars and bars. As I drifted closer to his waterfront, I noticed the shape was a drawing of Jesus. What could that mean? It dawned on me that the Religious Right was so blissfully unaware of American history that they probably thought Jesus had helped the South win the Civil War." When I introduced Jen, the fans did applaud wildly.

People attending these events were entertained and amused. Not so a far-right website called *Newsbusters* that called AU a "secular left group" and blasted us for being involved with Sarah Silverman, who was the creator of an "infamous" skit poking fun at God. I've seen that skit and it is more about self-deprecation and her inquiries about God and the universe, but I realize that Big Questions like that are a bit beyond the Right's understanding. The website then went on to condemn our promotion of Catie Curtis and Melissa Ferrick at a concert the next night at the Church of the Epiphany in downtown Washington because they had performed at (gasp!) "a gay-left event celebrating the first Obama inauguration in 2009."

In its third season we had a show at the legendary Club Passim in Harvard Square in Cambridge, Massachusetts that featured all transgender musicians. By this time, after losing their battle to stop "same sex marriage" at the Supreme Court, the Religious Right had turned its attention to hateful recriminations against transgender persons with all kinds of pseudoscience and political horror stories, along with promotion of "bathroom bills" that would prohibit entry to gender specific bathrooms to persons who were not that gender at birth. They wanted all Americans to fear what would happen if "gender identity" were the key to enter those facilities. Turned out there was nothing to fear at all. Law enforcement officials in twelve states that have gender identity as the basis of bathroom entry have found no cases of harassment or assault by transgender people. A survey by the Williams Institute found that 70% of transgender persons had suffered harassment or violence while trying to use a restroom. Women have more to fear from strange men coming into the bathroom.

On the political front, the Right began obsessing over "gender unicorns," which Franklin Graham said on a Christian radio show were creeping into the Charlotte-Mecklenburg school district in North Carolina. The Trans Student Educational Resources Group created an educational resource to help all people understand gender identity to help curb bullying. Graham, though, saw only a nefarious plot to push the normalizing of transgender folks. He seemed to think that without modest affirmation, transgender people would not even exist. In this view, he seemed to be channeling the words of former Iranian despot/President of Iran Mahmoud Ahmadinejad who, while giving a lecture at an American university a few years earlier, asserted that gay people do not exist in his country.

Catie thought Passim would be a great venue to do a session of Voices United devoted entirely to music by transgender musicians. She was a friend of Faith Soloway, one of the creators of the award-winning Amazon series *Transparent* based in large part on the experience Faith and her sister Jill had growing up and finding a parent "coming out" at the age of seventy. In the series Jeffrey Tambor is an aging father who transitions from Mort to Maura. *Transparent* was slated to be a Broadway show, but Tambor's problems involving sexual harassment delayed the project. Faith did a few songs on the piano and Catie asked her some questions and took inquiries from the audience. I met members of the Butterfly Music Transgender Chorus and Cici Eberle, who I later interviewed on my short-lived podcast. I also gave a little speech about what AU was doing to protect LGBTQ+ rights in lobbying efforts and litigation. There was a Harvard professor in the audience who taught storytelling there. I will admit I never thought of storytelling at Harvard, which I usually associated with quantum physics and Latin American history, but I'm glad it's there. She said I was a good storyteller.

Catie Curtis continued to be a part of my life long after those iconic concerts were over. She volunteered to sing at my retirement party in 2018; did a set at our "moving" party as we left Maryland for a townhouse in Washington DC; and participated in a service at the hundredth anniversary of the Community Church of Boston in April of 2020, contributing a new song about the silence of the streets of Boston in the midst of the coronavirus calamity and a remembrance of the Boston Marathon bombings that occurred near the church. Catie has given up much of the life of a traveling musician to become a therapist. I can't imagine anyone doing a better job of counseling than Catie.

Through the Voices United for Separation of Church and State project and my love of acoustic/folk/folk-rock/progressive country music, I've met many terrific performers. I'll highlight two who deserve more widespread acclaim.

Voices United Concerts

Since 2012, more than 120 Voices United concerts have taken place across the United States, raising awareness and support for Americans United for Separation of Church and State. The artists shown here are just some of the hundreds who have performed these concerts. The events help Americans United lobby, litigate, organize and educate in support of its core mission – protecting Americans from government-imposed theology and defending the fundamental right of conscience. Want to help? Contact Catie Curtis at curtis@au.org.

www. au.org

Some of the hundreds of performers who helped us raise funds for Americans United. Bianca De Leon is in the middle of the left side; Tom Pacheco is at the bottom left corner.

Tom Pacheco

Tom Pacheco is the greatest living American songwriter. Country artist Steve Earle once said that Texas songwriter Townes Van Zandt was the greatest and that he would dance on Bob Dylan's coffee table and say that to Bob's face. I beg to differ, but perhaps Steve Earle never heard Tom Pacheco. This would not be surprising because Tom is, like many prophets, less respected in his own country than he should be.

I first heard a Tom Pacheco record when he was performing as a duo with Sharon Alexander. That duo did one fine album and then disbanded. He was then signed to a solo contract with RCA, but in the early Seventies, that label dropped most of its male singer-songwriters, apparently convinced that James Taylor was enough for everybody. Tom went on to other and smaller labels and produced fifteen beautiful albums. Prior to the internet, many of these were hard to find, but on occasional trips to Scandinavia, I'd come across these CDs, often as prominently displayed in record stores as those of Willie Nelson and Dolly Parton. They were a brilliant collection of political songs, love songs, humorous songs, and historical portraits of people as diverse as Che Guevara and Jack the Ripper.

What was strange to me was not just that I never heard his music on the few "folkie" radio programs, but that I never had a chance to see him. Living in Boston and later in Washington, DC, where there were plenty of listening rooms with similar performers, he never appeared anywhere.

By the time Voices United started, the internet was full-blown. I located a woman named Nancy Stitham who was booking gigs for Tom. When I first expressed confusion about why I had never been able to see Tom perform in Washington, she explained that "people have to ask performers to perform."

So, I asked. I had a lengthy chat with him on the phone a few weeks before the scheduled "house concert" and found his passion and story-telling ability on the telephone as powerful as his songs on CDs. The Saturday night of his performance he arrived in the late afternoon in a car driven by his friend, Fred Kurland. It turned out that Tom rarely drove. Nancy came from New York City where she was a public-school teacher to see the show and mentioned that Tom had spent days putting together his play list for the evening. The show was spectacular, with comments that included one from a local minister who said, "He literally is a prophet for our times" and a neighbor who characterized him as "the most powerful singer" she had ever heard. He sold a large number of CDs, which is a way that traveling musicians of that era made more than what they were paid by hosts or club owners.

We became close friends after that show and I would try to see him whenever possible, including occasionally in Woodstock where he lived and where I would go for fundraising purposes. He seemed to have stories about everyone in the New York Greenwich Village folk scene, as well as writers in the Seventies acoustic music world of Los Angeles. His memory was encyclopedic. For example, he recalled the first time he saw country singer Emmylou Harris, "She took my breath away as she walked in the door in a white coat with the guy she was dating at the time, Paul Siebel." He brushed off my fascination with how many people he knew by noting that "the music business is pretty small." In his Greenwich Village apartment, people like Phil Ochs and Eric Andersen would sometimes sleep on the floor.

Tom wrote the only song that guarantees I will cry when I hear it: "Juan Romero." Juan was the kitchen worker from Mexico who was in the iconic photograph holding the head of Robert F. Kennedy after he was shot by Sirhan B. Sirhan in the kitchen of Los Angeles' Roosevelt Hotel on June 5, 1968, after he had just won the Democratic primary in California against Senator Eugene McCarthy. Romero gave Kennedy his set of rosary beads as he lay dying. The song describes how from that night forward Romero "wished he had taken the bullets himself." Tom had worked in the Kennedy campaign and was outside the Roosevelt celebrating until he heard the news of the assassination.

Juan Romero had never visited Kennedy's grave at Arlington National Cemetery. A few years before Romero's death in 2019, a reporter from the The Los Angeles Times named Steve Lopez did a feature on Romero's one and only visit to the gravesite. Tom had helped the two get in touch.

Bianca De Leon

Bianca De Leon may be the greatest unheralded female singer-songwriter. As with Tom Pacheco, I found her CDs in used record stores and in Europe. Listening to the very first CD of hers in a car CD player, I thought "Every one of these cuts is great. I wonder if she is still alive." The second half of that thought was prompted by the significant number of songs about drugs, drug dealers, and violence. I was afraid she may have succumbed to a gunshot or an overdose. The internet existed by the time I heard that first CD, but for some inexplicable reason, I never tried to find out anything about her that wasn't in the spare liner notes of her albums. In fact, one of her albums, a live recording from Helsinki, Finland, only used her first name *Bianca*.

Imagine my surprise the first time I went to the big convention of folk artists and enthusiasts sponsored by the Folk Alliance International, held that year in Memphis, Tennessee. Many artists had small showcases in rooms in a section of one of the conference hotels. These went well into the early morning hours. You could find out who was performing by looking at a little booklet distributed by the group. At 1 a.m., there was a listing for Bianca De Leon. I got there and found Bianca. She looked like her picture on one of her albums. After listening to her set, I introduced myself and said, "I'm really glad to see you; I thought you were probably dead." She laughed, gave me a copy of her brand-new CD, and then said she had to get to her next show at 2 a.m. a few floors away. She also asked me if I'd carry her guitar there. I listened to that set also, hearing more great music, and we snacked on some of the food found in those rooms and agreed to have breakfast the next morning.

Bianca explained that so many of her songs were based on actual events in her life. One of my favorite songs was "I Sang Patsy Cline the Night Noriega Fell." This chronicled her return to Texas after visiting her drug-dealing boyfriend in Colombia. The plane had to stop in Panama City. Before it could take off again, the lights in the airport went out. The flight was canceled. She had no place to stay and could hear gunfire in the distance. Getting a lift from a few men who had an apartment in the city, she found out the United States government had chosen that night to take out President Manuel

Noriega, a thorn in the side of then President Ronald Reagan. When she got to the apartment, she could hear gunshots all night and, as she kept close to the walls of the place, she started humming the tunes of Patsy Cline: "I Fall to Pieces" and "Walkin' After Midnight." Thus, the song was born.

Bianca's manuscript *Wild Ride* chronicles so many of the stories I heard from her that weekend we first met. She was once sleeping in a cornfield when she heard members of the Ku Klux Klan burying an African American man they had just murdered. Perhaps the most bizarre tale, though, was when she was young and hitchhiking through California. She accepted a ride with a young couple who had already picked up another hitchhiker they just called "Charlie." She and Charlie did not get along and at one convenience store stop, he tried to lock her out of the car. That night she decided to terminate her hitching relationship and just left the place they were all sleeping. A few weeks later she saw a picture on the front page of a local paper with a photograph of "Charlie." It gave his last name, "Manson," and told of his arrest for the murder of several Hollywood celebrities including actress Sharon Tate.

I was correct to be worried that she might have been killed. She also had plenty of boyfriends who were involved in the drug business in the United States and South America, one such relationship chronicled in her song, "My Boyfriend Got Shot."

She did a few benefits for Americans United, including a gig at an El Paso art museum and at our house in Maryland. She is still writing and recording new music, but like Tom, it is easier for her to find jobs and sales in Europe.

Tom and Bianca are perhaps the two best examples of songwriters who, in my view, ought to be better known. I can't list all the other artists who helped us and are in that category, but here are a few: David Wilcox, Cheryl Wheeler, Anne Hills, Grant Peeples (who didn't play in public until he was forty years old), and Darryl Purpose (who walked across the United States in the 1986 Great Peace March and was a professional poker player). And so many more. To this day, when I hear that any of the more than 100 artists who helped us are playing somewhere near where I am, I try to go see them perform.

Aessman 2017

Barry Lynn, Tom Paxton, and Joanne Lynn.

Chapter 9

AND THEN THERE ARE MOVIES

My memoirs have numerous references to movies. I love them. I can get into classics like films of Godard and Kurosawa, but my heart is happiest when it is watching horror movies. Even the most cheaply made ones are usually worth at least one viewing. I had the good fortune of meeting a legendary "creature creator" whose name is not terribly well-known but should be. Orson Welles directed 13 feature films; Steven Spielberg directed 33. David DeCoteau has already directed roughly 125 and he is only 60.

As streaming of movies became more popular, many people decided they were done with "physical media," like DVDs and even Blu-Rays. Many DVD rental chains disappeared, including Family Video, Blockbuster, and some branches of Rasputin Records. There was a closing of a Rasputin branch near Mountain View, California in 2011. Still collecting physical discs, I cleaned up as the discounts got deeper every day of my week's trip there.

I have a bucket list that includes seeing every feature film ever made anywhere in the world. Even with COVID-19 video watching, I may miss a few. At Rasputin, there was a major effort to stock cult films, motion pictures designed to get a loyal viewership in a genre and not generally able to attract more mainstream audiences. On my jaunts there, I tended to get J-Horror (Japanese) films and anything with a monster as its centerpiece. In the latter category, I bought *Grizzly Rage* and *Mammoth*. The former is a tale of high-school graduates who take a last fling to the woods post-graduation but then run over a grizzly bear cub entering the forest. Mama Bear is not pleased.

Notwithstanding that the actors and actresses appeared to have failed five or more grades and thus had aged out of traditional high-schoolery, and that the grizzly mother was seen almost entirely as an animatronic head constantly growling, there was something pleasant about what the director had achieved with an obviously limited budget. I didn't pay attention to who that director was. *Mammoth* had the premise of a previously stuffed mammoth in a museum awakened by a meteor explosion. It seemed decidedly less well directed, even though the premise was more interesting than the one in *Grizzly Rage*.

Joanne and I flew back from visiting our son near San Francisco to Boston for Thanksgiving with our daughter. Since Joanne needed to speak in New York City, we decided to take the train from Boston to DC; she could decamp in New York City, and I'd go on to Washington. Carrying all those DVDs (and a portable DVD player), I figured I could watch a few on the way home.

The day I returned, I was working from home and had put all the DVDs on a stack near my computer. I was delaying whatever I was supposed to be doing and fooling around on social media, which for me at the time was almost entirely checking on Facebook. I used to get a few requests for friendship every day, and most were from people I didn't remember knowing in real life. The ones from women who had a picture and a posting on their Facebook page of something like "Free Nudes Here," could be skipped. That morning I got a request from someone named "David DeCoteau." It was an unusual name that I vaguely recognized. I Googled him and found that he was a director of a large number of horror films, including the film I had just watched on that train trip the night before, *Grizzly Rage*. I figured he was asking me to be a Facebook friend.

I accepted his friend request and wrote that I had just viewed one of his films on the previous afternoon. His response came quickly: "Which one?" Me: "*Grizzly Rage*." David: "Not one of my best." We had a few more exchanges and a telephone call so that he could verify that I was a true horror fan and the guy who appeared on some cable shows he watched. We had a nice conversation for about twenty minutes, and he said that if I came to Los Angeles, he'd like to show me some of the great horror movie sites and take me to lunch. This sounded like great fun, and, when I went to Los Angeles a few months later, I arranged for us to have lunch at a popular luncheonette.

We had a good lunch, and he then ran into another film buff and writer, David Del Valle. The two Davids started talking about a vast number of low budget movies. I didn't say anything except hello until they seemed to be slowing down. I piped up: "Great conversation. I suspect I'm the only person who not only has heard of all those movies but has seen 95% of them." They seemed impressed.

On the next leg of the day, I drove around Hollywood listening to David (DeCoteau) describe exciting filming locations for *Rock N Roll High School* with the Ramones, the sound stage where Tor Johnson and Bela Lugosi battled a rubber octopus in *Bride of the Monster*, and the houses Jamie Lee Curtis fled from and later returned to in the first *Halloween*.

A year later, I was again in Los Angeles for a board meeting of a small arts foundation on which I sit. David was having his more or less annual Scream Queen Festival at Dark Delicacies in Burbank, California, and as soon as I broke from business, I took a cab to Burbank. It was raining and the traffic was lighter than anything I've ever seen in Los Angeles. When I arrived, the crowd was substantial, all there to see the actresses, actors, and directors signing their photographs, books they had written, and videos they were selling.

What an astonishing collection of Hollywood heroines (and a few heroes), including Linnea Quigley, Brinke Stevens, and Michelle Bauer—probably the best-known trio of "Scream Queens" in B-movie history. William Lustig, director of *Maniac Cop* was there, and Eileen Dietz, the stunt double for Linda Blair in *The Exorcist*, who did a notorious masturbation scene because Linda was too young. That evening David took me to dinner and regaled me with stories of his filming.

At one of David's later festivals, I ran into a playwright and filmmaker named Samuel Joseph. He recognized me from my frequent MSNBC and CNN guest appearances, and we became good friends. He directed a very clever film about the corruption of wealth called *Window of Opportunity* and wrote a play for Ed Asner to play God and mediate between two pundits, a conservative woman and a liberal man, about the state of affairs in the country. Prior to the COVID-19 calamity, I was working with Sam and Ed's daughter to see if we could launch a production of this in Washington. Regrettably, Ed died in 2021 and the play seemed unlikely to be performed again.

In 2014, David's Scream Queen event hosted the highest number of his collection of actors and actresses ever, including adult film actress Ginger Lynn. Ginger has been ranked #7 in a list of greatest adult film actresses of all time by *Adult Video News*. I had never met her during the Porn Commission days but always found it curious that, when I was interviewed for the network news, there was frequently a clip of a movie marquee showing a film with Ginger Lynn, Amber Lynn, or Porsche Lynn. I could almost hear viewers thinking: So are those actresses Barry's sisters? As a person who knows when a fan is spending too much time chatting with me, I could tell that Ginger had been trapped behind her signing table by a super-fan. I hated to do it, but I interrupted their conversation and introduced myself. Her fan quickly departed, and I was able to tell her about my work against the Meese Commission. She signed a photograph to Joanne that said: "I am not related to your husband." She also mentioned that she had been in a federal prison for a while because she had refused to cooperate with federal authorities investigating the case of Traci Lords. (Traci Lords was only seventeen when she made a number of hardcore pornographic films and this technically constituted child pornography.)

Chapter 10

NON-PROFITS AND CELEBRITIES

I was involved in two major Americans United events involving Hollywood celebrities and musicians. The first was First Freedom First, a joint venture with the Interfaith Alliance, funded for two years by Andy Grove, the founder of Intel. He had convinced a fellow philanthropist to match his one million dollar grant to Americans United and the Interfaith Alliance for a two-year project to support the separation of church and state.

Andy had a reputation for getting advice from the person doing the work he was interested in, rather than from a supervisor in the Intel chain of command. The Grove Foundation included his wife and daughter (active in local Planned Parenthood activities) and we would gather in their modest offices for a day of business planning. At the time, Andy was suffering from a severe form of Parkinson's that left his sharp mind intact but increasingly made mobility difficult.

We created a project called First Freedom First, complete with a book of that title and a motion picture called *Everything You Ever Wanted to Know about Separation of Church and State...But Were Afraid to Ask* (a play on the name of a popular book and Woody Allen movie in the Seventies). Hosted by actor and frequent documentary film narrator Peter Coyote and produced by Adam Klugman, the son of actor Jack Klugman, the idea was to highlight eight areas that were battle zones for current "anti-church state separation" efforts, including "Worship...Or Not" and "Sound Science." The culmination of the project was a show to be recorded live one evening at a theater in Washington, edited overnight, and then aired in movie theaters the next day.

The whole program featured celebrities interested in our issues and champions of the cause who put themselves at risk by challenging unconstitutional initiatives of governments or defying the Religious Right (or both).

Adam's father was the great actor Jack Klugman. Jack was convinced to come to Washington for two days for rehearsal and taping. Jack was on a hit television series called *The Odd Couple* with Tony Randall, but I had been a fan since his work in the courtroom drama *Twelve Angry Men* and several episodes of *The Twilight Zone*. When I first met Jack, he told me how he loved how I'd "kicked the ass" of Kentucky Senator Bill Frist over Frist's claim that he had, as a physician, diagnosed that Ms. Terri Schiavo was in a coma from which she could recover. His diagnosis and prognosis of possible recovery came solely from watching some videos of Ms. Schiavo from his office in Washington—1,000 miles from the subject being assessed—which is not known as a reputable medical diagnostic technique.

Other actors who helped us were Wendy Malick of the television show *Just Shoot Me!* and Dan Luria of the hit series *The Wonder Years*. At a dinner after the rehearsal, Dan reminded me that television networks were now ignoring positive portrayals of common vocations, noting that in the Sixties there were two popular television shows about teachers including the popular *Room 222*. He thought the networks were missing out on exploring important issues by focusing so much time on legal and medical programs.

Kevin Bacon is one of my favorite actors and he joined the program to do a few songs with his brother. I'd seen The Bacon Brothers perform at music clubs and the Philadelphia Folk Festival. He wasn't talkative prior to the show or in comments afterward. I didn't realize until he told Howard Stern on his radio show that he was not comfortable speaking extemporaneously and that he felt much better memorizing a script. He was a big draw for our sold-out audience and didn't fail any of us with his contribution to the program.

The emcee was noted actor Peter Coyote, whose golden voice also makes him the greatest narrator of documentaries since

Orson Welles, and we talked about many things including his years at a Buddhist retreat and the assassination of John F. Kennedy. He happened to mention that he was reading this "great book about the dumbing down of America" but he couldn't remember the title. .... When I asked him if it could be *The Age of Unreason,* he said that was it. I told him he'd be interviewing its author Susan Jacoby a few hours later. Small world confirmed again.

Comedian Marc Maron did some stand up and a segment where he asked questions of audience members. I had met Marc when he had me sit in once on his three-hour politics and comedy show on Air America. To sit in, I had to go to New York the night before the show which began at 6 a.m. and the arrangements started at 5:30 a.m.

The film was eventually shown in thirty-seven cities and was turned into the DVD *Everything You Ever Wanted to Know About Separation of Church and State...But Were Afraid to Ask.* One of the top donors to Americans United, Bob Goodrich, ran a large chain of multiplexes in the Midwest and gave us access to one theater in each of them. I drove to Richmond, Virginia, to watch in a theater there, accompanied by my daughter who was attending law school at the University of Virginia.

The segments highlighted sheroes and heroes of the separation cause, many of whom had heard of their colleagues in arms but had never met them. At the post-rehearsal dinner, I made a few remarks, starting with an observation once made by the Reverend Paul Kittlaus that, "These are the people I'd be happy going to jail with."

I'm sure that there are plenty of actors and actresses who can wax intelligently on many topics, but I know two on the top of my list: Matthew Modine and Richard Dreyfuss. My first meeting with Matthew was at a fundraiser for Americans United given by the Salon/ Sanctuary Series, whose artistic director Jessica Gould was a fan of church/state separation. Called "Between Heaven and Earth," the program of baroque music featured the Clarion Society Orchestra, two soloists, reading of letters between Thomas Jefferson and his beloved paramour in Paris, Maria Cosway, and some of his letters on religious freedom. Jefferson was played by Matthew Modine. Melissa Errico, who has one of the most gorgeous voices in music, played Maria. I gave a little speech when the event was ending to link Jefferson to some of the current church/state controversies. It went very well, and Matthew said he'd like to help us out in the future. He did.

Matthew had mentioned that he was directing some short films and was looking for venues to screen them. I have been a supporter of the American Film Institute for many years, and they have a marvelous tri-plex in Silver Spring, Maryland, right outside of Washington. They seemed more than willing to help host a screening, and we arranged one with Matthew and a few of my Washington political friends, along with a post-screening panel discussion. The panel featured then-director of the Washington Office of the ACLU, Laura Murphy, conservative radio host Janet Parshall, and Bob Edgar, former Congressman and now head of Common Cause. After I introduced Matthew, making references to several of his movies, he thanked me and said he'd like to take me with him to do introductions anywhere he spoke. After the event, he and a friend from California who was working in Washington, Ava DeMille, along with Joanne and me, sat around for hours talking politics and culture. Matthew ran twice to be the President of the Screen Actors Guild and, although I am not a member of that union, I thought he'd be grand at that job. He is truly a "renaissance person."

Speaking of references to movies, I was a participant in a celebration of the anniversary of the Religious Action Center of Reform Judaism, whose director, Rabbi David Saperstein, was one of the first religious activists I met when I got to Washington. The emcee that night was actor Richard Dreyfuss. I was honored to be invited to address the prominent role the Center had played in some many of the religious freedom debates over the decades I had worked with David.

I had been stuck for hours in an airport trying to get a flight to San Antonio, Texas, and began toying with the idea of incorporating some reference to each of Dreyfuss' films in my seven-minute speech. There were easy possibilities: *The American President* and *Whose Life Is It Anyway?* were two of his best-known works, but I told the audience that, when I realized the last film I had seen him in was *Piranha 3D*, I abandoned the project. Dreyfuss was there in part to promote his new non-profit to reinstate civics education in schools. Called the "Dreyfuss Initiative," its purpose is "to teach our kids how to run our country with common sense and realism before it is time for them to run the country. If we don't, someone else will run it and the experiment of government by, for, and of the people will have failed."

At the pre-program reception, I had also run into Al Franken who had recently been elected to the Senate from Minnesota, a man I used to see at Religious Right gatherings when he was trying to get comic material for his books and comedy appearances. We chatted about how strange it was to see the same kind of people that were at those conferences in the Nineties now roaming the halls of Congress with a Tea Party banner waving metaphorically over their heads.

IN CLOSING

This volume has told the stories from my early life and the extremely valuable opportunities given to me by my first major employer, the United Church of Christ. As this book closed, I took note of several interests that started in those years but became more significant at later points in my career.

In the second book in this series, I will tell the tales of my years fighting censorship while working for the American Civil Liberties Union and share my perspectives on some of the journalists I encountered during my ACLU days and beyond.

The third book in this series will report on my trials and triumphs defending the First Amendment as leader of Americans United for the Separation of Church and State.

About the Author

Barry W. Lynn caused lots of good trouble. He worked in Washington from 1974 to 2017–first for the United Church of Christ (UCC), helping gain amnesty for Vietnam war resisters and trying to stop registration for the draft; then for the ACLU, defending the First Amendment and destroying the Meese Pornography Commission; and finally for Americans United for Separation of Church and State, doing battle with every Religious Right leader aiming to have government adopt their agendas. Lynn is an ordained minister in the UCC and a lawyer with membership in the Supreme Court Bar.

Go to Barry Lynn's website *https://barrywlynn.com* to see videos and where he's speaking.

Index

E

F

G

M

N

O

P

Project Fair Play 137
Proxmire, William (Senate) 64
Puffin Foundation 150-151
Purpose, Darryl 173
Pyne, Joe 146

Q

Quote of the Day 24, 111-112

R

Ramirez, Mark Anthony 156
Ramsey, Nancy 97
Ransom, Louise 56, 69, 71
Rawls, Lou 118
Reagan, Ronald (President) 101, 114, 123-129, 173
Red Skelton 11
Religious Right 9, 14, 152, 155, 167, 180, 183, 187
Revolutionary Communist Party 124
Reyes, Alex 121, 127
Richards, Cecile 150, 151
Richey, Kim 138
Rivers, Joan 152
Robbins, Tony 139
Roberts, J. Milnor 98, 99
Robertson, Pat 15, 137
Rostker, Bernard 101-102, 103, 107, 112, 119, 121, 126-127
Rostow, Eugene 100
Rubendall, Howard 19, 148
Ruse, Michael 16
Ryan, Leo (House) 84, 85, 86

S

Salonen, Neal 86, 110, 111
Saperstein, David 182
Sasway, Ben 130, 131
Schapp, Bill 142
Scheer, Robert 35
Schempp, Ellery 164
Schiavo, Terri 180
Schlafly, Phyllis 103
Schmucker, Mark 132
Schroeder, Patricia (House) 93-95, 105, 108, 113
Schultz, Ed 155
Schultz, Larold K. 79
Schwab, Donald 76
Schwarzschild, Henry 57, 71
Scientology/scientologists 86, 106, 153
Scott, Eugenie 16

T

Ingram Content Group UK Ltd.
Milton Keynes UK
UKHW020904040423
419625UK00016B/1078